PLAIN GREEN WRAPPER

A Forester's Story

RONALD J. McCORMICK
FORESTER

"...One could do worse than be a swinger of birches."

– Robert Frost

DEDICATION

To my children, grandchildren and great grandchildren:
– A glimpse into my life and career -

And

To the men and women of the U.S. Forest Service, past and present, who continue to do their very best in 'caring for the land and serving the people'…my unequivocal admiration and respect.

ACKNOWLEDGMENTS

I have worked on these memoirs in fits and starts since 1990.

Through it all my wife, Carol, and my mother, Fran, have provided me encouragement to see it through to completion. Over that time Carol has been my reviewer, critic and chief editor. Often her memory of certain events was clearer than mine.

Thank you, Mom, for pointing me toward a career in forestry, and lately for supporting my effort to tell the story. And especially you, Carol, for your willingness and persistence in editing, and your gentle way of urging me to repeatedly rewrite to say it clearer and better, and to make it less a bureaucratic narrative and more a story.

CONTENTS

A NOTE FROM THE AUTHOR

A ll of us have led interesting lives. We all have a story. The chapters of my life are irrevocably tied to my assignments during my career with the U.S. Forest Service.

I originally intended my story to chronicle the last few years of my career. At the time of my retirement in 1990, the most recent years seemed the most important and relevant – certainly they were the most demanding, exciting and trying.

Now, years later, recollections of the early years in some ways seem richer to me; at least those years were more about being a forester. They were full of simple experiences, like finding a long-forgotten section corner from the original 1800s government land surveys, backpacking into the remote Mokolume River canyon for a surface rights survey, laying out a road or timber sale using aerial photos – far beyond roads in the rugged Mad River country of remote Northern California – and locating a route for the proposed Pacific Crest Trail high in the Eastern Sierra Nevada. What a career, what a life!

This project of writing memoirs is at least partly egocentric. Wanting to leave a record of what my life was about and what it may have contributed is certainly self-focused, but there is more to it than that.

The other motivation is for the benefit of my children, Shannon, Mike, Dan, Todd and Trina all of whom both suffered and benefited from my career moves and the trials of relocation. I hope this offers them some insights and understanding. My professional career was unusual and event-filled, and I hope the story will be of interest to them and my growing cadre of grandchildren. The story might also mean something to Forest Service employees and retirees.

Through it all, my admiration of the U.S. Forest Service as an organization and my great respect and deep affection for the men and women of this agency will be obvious.

I am unabashedly proud of my thirty-three-year career. I did my best to serve the public owners of the national forests, sought to make a positive difference in natural resource protection and management, and be a good leader. I also strived to be of help to my fellow employees and their career ambitions.

There is an in-house joke that describes a long time, dedicated Forest Service employee as one who wears green underwear. In my case, I believe I arrived swaddled in a Plain Green Wrapper.

CHAPTER ONE

Assignment Siskiyou

In late December 1979, my career in the U.S. Forest Service had led me and the family to Portland, Oregon. I was the Assistant Director for Outdoor Recreation for Region 6, the Pacific Northwest Region of the Forest Service, comprised of nineteen national forests located in Washington and Oregon.

I had now been in the position for three and a half years. My bride, Carol, worked in the regional office as the Business Management Assistant for the Directors of Land Management Planning and Program Development and Budget. The office building was the former old Multnomah Hotel, converted to office space, and located in downtown Portland. We commuted to work together every day.

We were living in a modest but comfortable home in the outskirts of Portland. Carol liked her job, and her colleagues and directors thought well of her. The kids, Todd, Dan and Trina were doing well in the excellent school system of Washington County. Our stay in Portland had been a positive one for the family.

One evening we had just finished dinner and Carol was cleaning up the kitchen. The kids were already downstairs doing homework or watching TV.

The phone rang and I grabbed it, a little irritated as always about evening calls. It was Jim Space, the Deputy Regional Forester. He quickly came to the point.

"Ron, sorry to call you so late, it's been a long and busy day." He sounded tired.

"No problem, Jim. What's up?" I replied.

"You were on the shortlist for the forest supervisor position on the Siskiyou National Forest, the chief has accepted our recommendation, and we're offering you the job."

I covered the speaker end of the phone and whispered excitedly to Carol, "The supervisor job on the Siskiyou!"

She smiled and nodded. I knew we didn't need to discuss it.

Jim went on. "If you'd like an opportunity to think about it, you can call me back in the morning."

"That won't be necessary, I accept," I said.

Jim was silent for a moment, and then laughed. "OK, Ron, contact Personnel about a house-hunting trip and prepare to report to the Siskiyou the end of October."

"Thanks, Jim. I really appreciate this, and I won't let you down," I replied, and we hung up.

It was normal in the Forest Service to take a day or even two to think about a job offer like this and discuss it with the family. However, Carol and the kids knew of and supported my aspirations. The Siskiyou National Forest and its headquarters in Grants Pass, located in southwest Oregon, was a desirable location. I had been chasing the goal of forest supervisor for so long; I just didn't want the opportunity to get away.

Carol and I were both pleased about the job offer. Todd, Dan and Trina understandably had mixed feelings. They liked the neighborhood and the schools and had developed a circle of friends. The bottom line was they were willing to go along with my career ambitions, and I appreciated their attitude.

I had been a district ranger at the age of thirty, and at the time I thought I had achieved my ultimate career goal in that most coveted position. Subsequent assignments to other national forests, first as a staff officer and then as a deputy forest supervisor, helped me decide I really wanted to be a forest supervisor. Suddenly I was forty-eight and in a regional office in a major city. I was running out of career time, and I felt it was now or never.

A year earlier I had entered the national competition for forest supervisor, arguably the second most coveted position in the Forest Service. Recently I had been on the chief's list for a national forest in the Southeast United States, and then for one in the Southwest. I was a bridesmaid for both, and I was beginning to think it was not going to happen.

Now, at last, I had been invited into that special circle of warriors to take my place at the roundtable with those chosen to protect and manage our national forests. I thought of it in those mystical terms of Camelot.

We listed the house with a realtor. Our plan was that Carol and the family were to remain behind then move following the end of the school term. We hoped the house would sell by then. I left for Grants Pass late in October, leaving the kids and Carol behind. I rationalized that without distractions I could really focus and concentrate on the new job.

It rained nearly every day that November of 1983. A cold, gray, seemingly never-ending Oregon rain that draped like a soggy blanket over my once-soaring spirit. I was staying alone in a large house on five acres I had rented in the countryside outside of town. I occupied just one of the four bedrooms. There was no real furniture yet, just a cot and sleeping bag, a two-drawer cardboard dresser that provided a place for a radio and lamp, and a straight-backed chair.

This should have been an exciting and happy time for me. I had just reached a major career goal, but the relentless rain and circumstances of our relocation were washing the joy out of it. This house felt so big, empty and cold.

Grants Pass was a picturesque, small town in southwest Oregon. I knew Carol and the kids would like it once they got here. It was clear to me, however, it would take a while to sell our house

– perhaps a long while. Interest rates were high, the real estate market slow, and buyer interest had been nil.

Bob Devlin, the supervisor of the nearby Rogue River National Forest, offered me some early advice. "Before you get tied down to administrative duties in the supervisor's office, get out and on the ground with the district rangers."

I arrived at the forest headquarters on October 31, 1983 – Halloween! Most of the technical and clerical help were in costume, and the mood on that day was light and cheerful. In my sport coat and tie I felt a bit out of step, but welcome. Someone asked me to help judge Halloween costumes and award prizes, and so I did. My first official ceremonial act!

I spent an initial couple of days with the staff and getting oriented to my new office. Then I acted on Devlin's advice and arranged to spend the next several weeks at the ranger districts, headquartered in the small towns that surrounded the forest.

Those visits facilitated the development of a relationship with each district ranger and gave me a better sense of the Siskiyou Forest. I asked the district rangers of Gold Beach, Powers, Cave Junction, Brookings, and Galice to arrange a 'family' meeting with all their employees. I had assumed they wanted to know what the new boss was like, and with over 350 employees, I had a lot of names and faces to learn. Over the course of a few weeks I visited each district in turn.

On intervening days I introduced myself to chambers of commerce, county commissioners, timber industry groups and environmental organizations in the communities. I set a demanding schedule, but so far I was satisfied that I was approaching this in a sound way, even though I was not yet sure how I was being received.

The toughest part was coming home after dark each evening to this cold silent house, which, coupled with the tension of beginning a new job, created emptiness in me. There was no one there to talk to, to unwind with and share the experiences of these first days. Thus I spent long evenings in that cavernous house listening to rain drumming on the roof and the strangled sound of water as it gurgled down clogged downspouts. I read background material on the Siskiyou National Forest. I reviewed information on the natural resources, issues and problems, budget, personnel, key people of the communities, and the political climate.

I had accepted this position and challenge enthusiastically and with eager anticipation, and on those long evenings alone there had been ample time for contemplation and introspection. In spite of knowing better, I would occasionally allow a bit of self-doubt to crawl from its dark place in the deep recesses of my brain back into my consciousness.

"Well, you've really done it now," I occasionally chided myself. I still thought of myself as that naïve, idealistic boy from a small town in northeast Ohio who loved to walk in the woods.

One evening while brushing my teeth and preparing for bed, I glanced in the bathroom mirror and saw a tired, haggard-looking person staring back at me.

"Wow, this has been a tough week," I said aloud, startled at the sound of my own voice.

"Well, this is what you wanted, isn't it?" the mirror replied. No sympathy there.

"Yeah, I guess so. Do you think I have what it takes?"

"Remember that you've prepared for this," the pale reflection responded. "Over the past twenty-five years you moved your family at least eight times across the western United States in a series of both lateral transfers and hard-won promotions to get to this time and place. Isn't this what you wanted and worked so hard to achieve?"

"Yes," I mused aloud. "We certainly have paid our dues."

I had served on seven national forests and one regional office in three states. These moves included pulling my first wife, Kaye, and our children out of their home state of California to Montana. That major relocation had been particularly disruptive and upsetting to Kaye, and difficult for our children Shannon, Mike and Dan.

I glared at the image in the mirror that was asking these tough questions. The person looking at me appeared older than I remembered, certainly tired and drawn. "You ask is this really what I want to do? Well, yes, it is," I said flatly. "Let's quit feeling sorry for ourselves and get on with it!"

I knew something was missing. I yearned for the support and reassurance of my family around me. I was more than ready for Carol and the kids to join me in Grants Pass.

It was getting late, but I called Carol anyway and whined. "Carol, I'm lonely and miserable, and what's worse, I'm beginning to talk to myself." I pleaded, "Please, pull the kids out of school and get on down here before Christmas!"

She understood my situation and finally agreed, if somewhat reluctantly. It meant the kids would be changing schools before the end of the school term, and she was concerned it could be academically disruptive. I was confident they could make the adjustment.

That was settled, and I felt a little better about my circumstances. As I lay in bed that night, seeking much-needed sleep, I reviewed what I had learned in the past few weeks about the dynamics of the Siskiyou, the employees and our publics.

The Forest Management Team and people of the Siskiyou were talented and demonstrated a solid 'land ethic'. They wanted to do right by the forest's natural resources. They seemed a bit dispirited, however – frustrated with the opposition, appeals and delays in moving forward with various forest projects. And it was clear they were accustomed to a top down, very directive management style.

I was also beginning to understand that the Siskiyou and Klamath Mountains were very unusual both geologically and floristically. Because of this, and their remoteness and wildness, these mountains had become a special, revered place for the environmental community. Yet they felt disenfranchised, excluded from the decision-making process and had resorted to formal appeals, lawsuits, confrontation and civil disobedience.

The timber industry sensed that a change in the general public's attitude about trees and timber harvest was developing, and were fighting for survival. They had established a 'fortress' mentality, and their first line of defense was political intervention. The two entities mostly communicated through acrimonious statements via the media. Sadly, the rest of the public appeared to be only mildly interested bystanders.

The stakes were high, battle lines drawn, and I knew I faced a serious and difficult test. This was not the idealized Camelot I had envisioned.

I finally drifted off into an uneasy, dream-like state. Scenes of the early years of my childhood drifted in and out of my consciousness. It had been a long and eventful journey that led me to this place and time, and the greatest challenge of my career.

New supervisor named for Siskiyou National Forest

Ronald J. McCormick has been named Supervisor of the Siskiyou National Forest headquartered in Grants Pass, according to Pacific Northwest Regional Forester Jeff M. Sirmon. McCormick, 48, will report to his new assignment Oct. 30.

He is now Assistant Regional Director of Recreation in the USDA Forest Service Regional Office in Portland, a position he has held since January 1980. He will replace Bill Covey, who transferred to Montana as Director of Timber Management for the Northern Region.

A native of Ohio and a 1958 forestry graduate of the University of Michigan, McCormick worked summers on National Forests in Idaho and California before receiving a permanent appointment in 1968.

McCormick's early career was spent in National Forests in California. He worked in timber management on the Stanislaus National Forest; was timber

Ronald J. McCormick

management assistant on the Mad River Ranger District, Six Rivers National Forest; was District Ranger of the Big Bear District of the San Bernardino National Forest; and was recreation staff officer on the Inyo National Forest from 1968 until 1974.

In 1974, he moved to Montana as Deputy Forest Supervisor of the Lolo National Forest. In that position, he was responsible for coordinating the Forest's timber management program with other forest resources. In 1976, he was assigned to the Wallowa-Whitman National Forest in eastern Oregon as head of the Hells Canyon National Recreation Area Planning Team. In 1980, he moved to his present assignment in Portland.

Accompanying McCormick in his move to Grants Pass will be his wife Carol and three children, Todd (15), Dan (14), and Katrina (12). The family also includes Mike, a college student in California, and daughter Shannon who lives in Baker.

First Day on the Siskiyou - Halloween!

CHAPTER TWO

The Early Years

S mall towns are great! That's just my opinion, of course. I had the good fortune to be raised in a small town. Cities, I learned early on, don't fit well with my personality and preferences; I seem to need open space, trees, and blue sky. I greatly dislike crowds, traffic, vast stretches of concrete and asphalt and constant city noises.

Chagrin Falls, Ohio remains a charming, rural town that was home for about 4,000 folks in the late 1930s and early 1940s. Mom, Dad and my younger brother, Jerry, and I lived in a modest two-story house with a full front porch that faced Bradley Street, which was lined with maple trees. The town is situated in the Chagrin River Valley, and the river flows through the heart of town with picturesque waterfalls both above and below the Main Street bridge. Most residents were acquainted with, or at least knew of, each other. Many worked in the local paper mill upriver or had service jobs connected with the community. It was an idyllic, Norman Rockwell kind of place to spend a childhood.

Dad – Homer Nelson McCormick – was lean and six feet tall. His face and arms were tanned from years of working outside. He was a handsome man, resembling the western actor of the day Randolph Scott. I admired his strong hands and forearms. He was usually quiet and easygoing but could be firm when he thought it was needed. He was raised in West Virginia and left school after the eighth grade to work. He demonstrated rather than taught my brother and me fairness, honesty and personal integrity. He was capable, conscientious and dependable – a man you could count on.

Over time he worked his way up from a lineman to a foreman position for the Cleveland Electric Illuminating Company and was in charge of the operation and 'line gang' that worked out of Chagrin Falls. They built high-tension steel towers, strung power-lines, and maintained the facilities, rights of way, and the power distribution network. Dad had no formal supervisory training, but it was clear to me his 'gang' both liked and respected him. He walked to work nearly year round carrying a lunch pail. Neighbors said they set their watch by Dad passing their house with his long strides on his way to work. Upon returning home, he always had sandwich scraps in his lunch bucket he had saved for the family dog.

Mom – Frances Virginia (Pinter) McCormick – made breakfast every morning for Dad, packed his lunch and got him off to work. She then made breakfast for Jerry and me and often packed us a lunch for school. In the evening she always had a nice supper ready which was served shortly after Dad arrived home; she was an outstanding cook. A petite, attractive woman with black hair, Mom was the foundation of the family and the catalyst that made it work. She provided a secure and caring home environment and did so with energy, intelligence, and resolve. Her other passion was cards, particularly bridge, and she had a reputation as an excellent player.

It was not so many years ago that Jerry and I learned that Mom had led a difficult childhood. Her father and mother were pioneer homesteaders in South Dakota and later Canada around the turn of the century; it was a hard life. Her mother died young, and Mom left home as a young teen to work and support herself and to finish high school. Her father did not value education and wanted her and her brothers to stay on the farm and work.

Mom was determined to provide a good home and caring atmosphere for our family. She strove to instill proper values in Jerry and me and to raise us well. She could be a bit direct at times, and some activities for us were mandatory.

"You will belong to the Methodist Church; attend Sunday morning services and Youth Fellowship in the evening." The way she said it left no question in our minds.

We joined Cub Scouts (Mom was a Den Leader), and later Boy Scouts (Dad was involved). Jerry achieved the rank of Eagle Scout. In general, we enjoyed a very loving, stable and predictable home life.

Mom has often told me the story of moving to our house on Bradley Street. I was two or three, and my brother Jerry had not yet been born. While moving in Mom noticed a boy, face pressed against the front windowpane, hands shielding his eyes from the glare. The small boy, with the sleeves of his too-large gray sweatshirt extending beyond his fingertips, came around to the front door and asked. "Do you have any kids?" It was Bruce Crittenden, and he lived a few houses up the street.

171 Bradley Street

Our address was 171 Bradley Street. The street was paved with red and orange bricks that had become a bit bumpy over the years. It was relatively short as streets go, ending on South Street about seven houses down, and on a gradual incline up a gentle hill it ended on a cross street about ten houses up. The grade was just steep enough to provide good sledding following winter snows.

Rows of mature sugar maples lined both sides of the street, their canopies overarching the street and creating a shaded, tunnel-like effect that provided deep shade in summer and a blaze of autumn colors in the fall. Most homes were the early 'Craftsman' style distinguished by broad wood decked front porches under a roof supported by concrete block or wooden columns. They were not elaborate nor pretentious, but solid, comfortable and inviting. During summer our front porch played host to neighborhood kids and countless games of checkers, monopoly and carrom.

Before the advent of television, the radio was the main source of family entertainment. We had a large Philco floor model. It was an impressive piece of mahogany furniture with a small lighted dial and a couple of control knobs near the top. Friday evenings were radio night. Dad would ask, "Who wants to listen to *Charlie McCarthy*?" He really liked that program.

Jerry and I would always be very receptive and eager for the event. Dad would tell Mom, "Get the boys a Pepsi, the program is about to start." We were allowed to enjoy a Pepsi once a week.

We would gather around this oversized console radio, Jerry and I usually sat or lay on the floor, and Mom and Dad made themselves comfortable in chairs close by. We listened to the simple plot and schemes of Charlie unfold and laughed out loud at his antics and jokes. Sometimes we listened to *Amos and Andy* for variety, and if we were lucky *Gang Busters*, a serial about J. Edgar Hoover and the FBI.

On Saturday mornings my assigned chore was to scrub the kitchen linoleum floor and the wooden steps leading to the basement. This was a bucket and rag, hands and knees job, and I did not appreciate it at all. I felt Jerry had the better deal in his assigned chore of dusting the dining room furniture.

I found a way to make the work bearable by listening to the little radio that was perched on a shelf in the kitchen. I listened to the *Lone Ranger* as I completed my chores, my head lost in the unfolding adventure of the Lone Ranger and 'his faithful Indian companion Tonto.' The musical theme, *Beethoven's Fifth Symphony*, still sends a chill through my body when I hear it and takes me back to the kitchen of our Bradley Street home. Time for the Lone Ranger!

'Smitty' was the chief of police of the three-man police force. He was a portly man of average height with a round, smiling face and kindly eyes. If I saw him downtown, he would say something like, "Good morning, Mr. McCormick, and how are things going for you today?" He seemed to know every kid in town, and we liked him. In retrospect, he was the most effective police officer I have ever known. There was little or no real crime in Chagrin Falls.

Coming out of the Great Depression times were lean. Dad had been fortunate to maintain steady employment, and he raised a large garden every summer. Mom canned all manner of vegetables and fruits, and we didn't seem to lack for anything.

Our cousin Gordon visited and stayed with us once in a while. He was being raised under different circumstances. He has since told Jerry and I more than once with admiration and envy in his voice, "You guys were just like the Nelson Family; you didn't know how lucky you were."

He was referring to the old TV sitcom *Ozzie and Harriet*. Remember David and Ricky? Gordon's visits afforded him another perspective, and he understood more than we that we were blessed. I didn't comprehend until much later in life that all childhoods were not like ours. Not that everything was perfect; we had our disagreements and conflicts, but overall it was a special home in a special place.

The consistency and predictability of that childhood experience affected me deeply. I still want breakfast at seven a.m., lunch at noon and dinner at six p.m. I am uncomfortable and irritable if it doesn't happen just that way. Geeze!

The Bradley Street Circus

The summers in Chagrin were often hot and muggy, and toward summer's end the neighborhood kids were running out of new things to do. We had played hide-and-seek, kick the can, and Monopoly on our front porch when it rained; we sought different entertainment. Mom was always a great one for thinking up activities to keep Jerry and I occupied. Perhaps her greatest brainstorm was a circus – our own circus!

It was 1946, and I was about eleven and Jerry was seven. I don't know from whence the inspiration sprang, but Mom announced to us one morning, "We are going to have a circus!"

I am sure we were dumbfounded. "What do you mean, Mom?" I asked.

"Well, all you children seem a bit bored, and I think we could all get together and have a backyard circus," she said. Then she added, "We could charge admission and donate it to the Milk Fund." There was a post World War II effort to provide milk to needy families.

Mom organized the production. She was always a great organizer. For our circus she enlisted other neighborhood mothers, including Bruce Crittenden's mom, and a few dads to help. We designed a one-ring circus, a 'fright house' in our garage, several acts, including a tightrope exhibition by Bruce Crittenden, a pair of performing midgets (Jerry McCormick and Gale Crittenden, Bruce's sister), a feature singer, animal trainers (the animals were family pets) and various acts by other neighborhood kids ranging in age from five to thirteen.

Mom also instructed us, "Circuses always have a parade to create excitement and drum up customers, so let's have a parade through the neighborhood." And we did. It was like a dress rehearsal; everyone was in costume and we paraded up or down every street in our end of town. We covered vast stretches of concrete and asphalt, drew a good bit of attention, and we soon had a group of kids trailing us.

The event went well. The press covered it, both local and Cleveland newspapers, and we had over a hundred people in attendance. We collected almost ten dollars, mostly by selling Kool-Aid and popcorn. That event tells much about Mom, the neighborhood, and the times than anything else.

Ober's Woods

Old man Ober, as we called him, owned a large amount of acreage consisting of a mosaic of pastures and hardwood trees and ran a few head of cows on his land. The 'woods' were located a distance beyond the railroad tracks, perhaps a thirty-minute walk away. Mr. Ober didn't seem to mind if kids from the nearby neighborhoods played there.

The woods were comprised of oak, hickory, beech and birch and were without roads. They were home to fox squirrels, red foxes, raccoons, crows and a variety of birds. They became both a continuing source of entertainment and inspiration, and sometimes for me a refuge. As a child of ten and into my early teens I would spend hours there, sometimes alone, sometimes with my neighborhood friends Bruce Crittenden, Bill Wendl and Roger Hartman.

The woods adorned hilly terrain, bisected by a small stream that at its source had rocky cliffs whose overhangs dripped water through the moss that clung to the porous rock. I appreciated the uniqueness and beauty of this place even then. Along the stream grew dense stands of slender, supple birch saplings. One of our boyhood activities was to climb one of these to the top, hang on tight and thrust out our legs and ride the sapling down to the ground as it yielded to our weight.

During one of these diversions I recall one of the guys, I think it was Bruce, on his ride down landing then falling into a yellow jackets' nest in the ground. The angry bees chased us down the creek and out into the middle of the pasture, biting us as we ran to anonymity and safety among the cows!

Many years later I read poet Robert Frost's wonderful poem *Birches*. A poem about a young boy living on a farm in the northeast whose source of play was the farm wood lot. He climbed the slender birch trees and rode them to the ground time after time. In my mind, Robert Frost captured the essence of our Ober's Woods, and what they meant to me as a young boy.

He concludes his poem by saying:

> *So was I once myself a swinger of birches.*
> *And so I dream of going back to be...*

My boyhood friends grew up and moved on to more traditional occupations, while I remained fixated on the woods. The start of my journey has its origins in Ober's Woods.

Hunt, Fish, and Trap

For as long as I can recall I loved to be outdoors. At the age of three I would wander off in whatever direction my interests took me. Sometimes I followed the family beagle, Jack, wherever his nose led him. Mom was forced to restrain me in the front yard (I vaguely recall being tethered to a tree). Mom had to call Chief Smitty more than once to help find me – I never knew I was lost.

There used to be advertisements in hunting and fishing magazines that featured correspondence courses on earning a living as a game warden and related occupations. The headline proclaimed with a bold banner: "Hunt, Fish and Trap for a Living". That notion fascinated me, and I think it planted the seed that germinated and slowly grew into a career ambition.

The notion was reinforced by Dad taking me rabbit, pheasant and squirrel hunting at an early age. Dad truly loved the fields and woods. He provided me with an early education on the ways of animals and instructed me on the use of firearms and ammunition. His childhood in West Virginia was highlighted by hunting, mostly as a way to augment the family's food supply. On Saturday mornings I recall him singing as he came downstairs, "*Way up on the mountain, where the squirrels are so many you can't count 'em.*" I guessed this was a refrain from an old country or folk song from his childhood.

Bruce Crittenden's father, Bruce Sr., often took me along with Bruce Jr. on fishing trips to local ponds and rivers. Bruce lived a few houses up our street, and we were childhood buddies and became lifelong friends.

As we grew older Bruce and I hunted and fished a lot together and also trapped muskrats (with an occasional raccoon, possum or skunk in the catch). Bill Wendl and Roger Hartman lived nearby and were usually a part of those activities. Near Ober's Woods, and across the railroad tracks, was a wet, swampy area, and the Chagrin River was just a short bicycle ride away. Our valley contained all the trees, plants, streams and wetlands necessary for a wide variety of wildlife and fish. This variety of habitats offered an intriguing environment for a young, outdoor-minded boy.

The Swamp

These wetlands and the pond were also a great attraction for me. We referred to this magical place as 'The Swamp'. It was a marshy area with a thick border of cattails surrounding a pond. In total it was comprised of three or four acres. It was alive with frogs, birds, muskrats, and all manner of insects. The spring and early summer were the best times. Bruce, Roger, Bill and I prowled its marshy edges and caught frogs. We marveled at the clouds of frog eggs that were suspended in the murky water, and later we were astonished by the thousands of tadpoles that developed from them. We witnessed their growth, and in a short time they grew legs, lost their tails, and became miniature frogs!

Roger Hartman's older brother trapped muskrats in the Swamp during the fall. I watched the process closely, and although trappers are typically secretive about the location of their 'sets' and methods, he was patient with his little brother's friends. He willingly educated Bruce and me on the art of trapping muskrats.

I learned that a trapper must take care to position the trap, chain and stake it in such a way that when the trap snapped closed, the startled muskrat bolted for deeper water. The weight of the trap and chain would cause the animal to sink and quickly drown. This was both humane and prevented the animal from twisting and chewing off the trapped appendage.

This was my introduction to a new world and adventure, trapping animals for their furs, stretching and drying the pelts on homemade stretcher boards and selling them. There was something special about wading into a pond or stream in early evening, reading signs of muskrat activity, carefully preparing a trap, then inspecting the sets at dawn. And oh the elation of a successful catch – a drowned muskrat!

The Swamp usually froze over by December. What an opportunity! My neighborhood companions and a collection of school friends would meet there on Saturday mornings. We would shovel the snow off the ice and build a first-class hockey rink. It was there we all learned to skate and enjoyed rousing games of hockey, even though hard falls and bruised butts were common.

We bought hockey sticks at the local hardware store and taped and painted them to create our own distinctive stick. Red and blue were my favorite colors. This was a big deal and great fun!

The Great Trapping Enterprise

As we grew older, Bruce and I ran a joint trap line. It was a serious endeavor for both of us. We acquired a book on trapping techniques, and from it we learned how to deodorize and remove the shiny metal sheen from new steel traps. We gathered the bark of various trees and shrubs as instructed, and with boiled water we concocted a vile brew in which to soak the shiny new traps. I was amazed our parents put up with the foul odor drifting up from our basements, but they did and the process worked. The traps stained to a dark bluish color that varied depending on the chosen ingredients, and they also lost their oily, metallic odor.

After a few seasons of running a joint trap line and sharing the meager profits, we decided to run our own independent lines. A properly dried muskrat pelt would fetch from one to four dollars depending on its size and condition. We thought there would be more profit if we each had our own line. We sold pelts to either a local buyer or sent them to Sears and Roebuck, which for many years purchased furs from independent trappers.

The notion of trapping wild animals for their pelts is likely distasteful or downright abhorrent to many. At this point in my life I would not argue the point, except to say that the experience provided a combination of character building, lessons in responsibility and an environmental education that influenced and shaped my life.

It required dedication and commitment for a sixteen-year-old boy to get up at five a.m. on a school day and run a trap line of twenty or so sets in the dark. I checked traps, flashlight in hand, by wading into the frigid waters of the Swamp, or paper mill pond, or Chagrin River, and often re-set or relocated them. More often than not I had nearly frozen fingers and very wet feet. I wore hip boots, but they either leaked, or I went over the top by sinking in mud or wading the rain-swollen river. I rushed home after school to skin the day's catch, and I stretched the hides, inside out, over thin boards to dry. Bruce and I had cut out and shaped boards just for that purpose. It was all hard work, but I loved it.

Bruce often called me in the early morning for a report. He would say something like, "I caught two 'rats', how did you do?"

I might reply that I only caught one.

Bruce would laugh and say, "Maybe you'll do better tomorrow." We enjoyed comparing results and techniques, although I must admit I think he was better at trapping than I.

Hunting

When I was very young, Dad would hunt with friends and often bring back game, which Mom would prepare for the table. We regularly ate fried squirrel, rabbit and, occasionally, a pheasant.

I was fascinated and couldn't wait to be old enough to go with him.

At the age of five or six, I begged to go with Dad on a rabbit hunt with Jack, our beagle. I promised to stay out of the way and just watch. Dad finally relented and took me along. After a morning of pushing and struggling through a field of dense weeds higher than my head, we returned home. Mom still delights in telling my reaction to her question, "Well, Ronnie how did you like it?"

She tells me my reply was, "All right I guess, but the hunting season kept hitting me in the face!"

In time, Dad gave me my first shotgun, an old Mossberg bolt action 410-gauge he purchased from one of his friends at work. Dad was very strict about gun safety, and he drilled me on the importance of not pointing a gun at anyone at anytime, even if I was sure it wasn't loaded. He required I check and recheck the gun's chamber and magazine to ensure I was not bringing a loaded gun into the car or house. In the field or woods he would periodically direct me, "Check your safety and make sure it is on 'safe'."

I learned from Dad how to travel quietly and unnoticed through the hardwood forests of northern Ohio. If I stepped on a brittle branch, and it emitted a loud "crack", he would glance at me but say nothing – words were not necessary. He showed me how to identify a squirrel's favorite hickory nut or beech tree by the abundance of fresh nut hulls on the ground. He taught me to wait quietly and patiently for a fox or gray squirrel to arrive.

On countless crisp fall mornings in the Ohio woods I would sit quietly and listen to the inhabitants stir and awaken. The tranquility would be interrupted by the crash of branches in the distance as a squirrel leapt from tree to tree, traveling towards its favorite breakfast tree.

Fishing

Dad loved to hunt but didn't care for fishing. Fortunately, Bruce's dad did. He was an expert with a fly rod and tied his own flies. He often took his son fishing and invited me along. Thus I acquired an interest and the knowledge of fishing early on, and I remain indebted to Bruce Sr. for his kindness.

A large reservoir on the Chagrin River provided water for the papermaking process of the local paper mill. A pipeline perhaps five feet in diameter, traversed the edge of the reservoir and provided an excellent pathway and platform from which to fish. We called it the 'Pipe'.

The cry, "Let's go to the Pipe and fish!" was often heard on summer days in the late 1940s. We jumped on our bicycles, with fishing rods lashed to them, and rode the two miles or so to a spot where we could access the pipeline. The pipe was getting old even then and often leaked in many places along its route. The big hazard was stepping around a spray of water shooting upward from a leak without falling into the reservoir.

The many leaks created wet areas on the landside of the pipe, allowing cattails and reeds to grow. It provided a habitat for an amazing variety of birds, large bullfrogs, muskrats and raccoons. The area teemed with wildlife, and I grew to love its naturalness. Now, when I return to Chagrin Falls, it becomes one of the places I must visit again.

We would catch bluegills, sunfish, sometimes a bass, and also fish for catfish at night. We even caught bullfrogs by using a patch of red flannel material on the hook and line of a cane pole and waving it in front of the frog. It worked! It was all great fun, a good way to spend the day, and we often supplied our families with fresh fish. Mom was always a good sport about cooking our fish and game, as long as we properly cleaned or dressed it.

Another favorite place to fish was a quiet pool of water below the Chagrin River waterfall in town. At its edge lay a large, elongated rock with a cleft or depression along its length. We named it 'Canoe Rock'. The rock was big enough for Bill, Bruce, Roger and I to sit in its interior depression and fish over the edge with a handline, sinker, hook and worm. When we ran out of worms, we turned rocks over and caught crawdads. Fish loved crawdad tails. We caught a lot of fish there, often to an audience of onlookers leaning on the rail of the Main Street bridge far above while they munched popcorn from the nearby Popcorn Shop. A staircase now enables people to reach the river and view the waterfall, and it has become a popular setting for weddings.

The Recreation Center

On hot summer days Bruce, Bill, Roger and I would grab our swimsuits, towels, and sack lunches, and take our secret trail, 'The Path', to the community swimming pool. The Path cut diagonally across woods and fields, making it a shorter route than following streets and roads through town to the pool.

The pool, complete with diving board, lifeguards, and a wading pool for toddlers, was located a mile or so from the center of town. It was in a complex that included the football field, track and concrete football stadium. The Recreation Center was a wonderful facility for its time; we did not fully appreciate how fortunate we were.

Unknowingly, the center also offered early education on the female anatomy. The changing rooms and lockers were located under the football stadium, and a concrete wall separated the boys' locker room from the girls'. Water pipes went through the walls at various places to the sinks and toilets on both sides, and some creative young man discovered he could enlarge the hole around the pipes by chipping away at the concrete. Some of these openings afforded narrow glimpses into the adjoining room. A revelation! We could take turns peering into the girls' locker room and watching nubile young ladies in various stages of dress and undress.

One summer afternoon High School Principal Ted Gurney entered the boys' locker room and caught a group of us in the act! Mr. Gurney was six feet five inches tall, and an appropriately stern principal. His face was red with anger, and with his huge right hand he grabbed the unfortunate peeping tom by his collar and escorted him forcefully out the door. The rest of us scattered like frightened quail. The next day the holes were repaired with a very hard material and our anatomy classes were suspended. I often wondered if future generations of boys – or girls – ever figured out how to revive this activity. I bet they did.

High School

The Chagrin Falls' school system built a reputation over the years of offering high-quality education and a complete athletic program. The school won national awards for excellence in both categories. During my high school years I didn't appreciate that fact, or I didn't pay much attention. I didn't always apply myself well in school and was just an average student.

I enjoyed athletics. Football, track and baseball were my best sports, and there are a few stories worth relating in that regard.

I played football in all four years of high school. I was only five feet ten inches tall and 150 pounds, but I had good speed and was not timid about hard physical contact. I thought I could be a good running back, as I had excelled as such in playground games. Our now legendary coach, Ralph Quesinberry, had other ideas. He wanted me to play on the line as a guard. He told me that he had two smaller and nearly as fast players that were too small to play on the line and that he could only utilize them in the backfield. Since our high school had a total of only two hundred students, the coach had to utilize nearly all the students who tried out for sports. In addition to playing guard on offence, the coach also wanted me to play defensive back. In other words, I was to play full time.

I was disappointed but played the positions he wanted. He was

33

the coach, and a good one, and it was a decision, not a suggestion. As a result, and in retrospect, I believe I played like I had something to prove. I played very hard all the time; I blocked and tackled with gusto against much larger players. After several hard tackles, I recall having trouble locating the huddle. As they say in the game, I had my 'bell rung.' My heritage from four years of high school football was a broken nose, broken right shoulder, and a split kidney.

Track is a more positive story. I liked to run and still do. Even in my late forties I ran in several 10,000-meter (10K) organized race events and placed well. Sprinting, however, was my forte. I have a box full of ribbons and medals won by my sprinting efforts in high school track. However, one goal eluded me, and therein lays another story.

In 1952, my junior year, and again as a senior in 1953, I placed second in both the 100-yard and 220-yard dashes (now the 100 and 200-meter dashes) in Ohio District track meets. I usually ran a close second behind John Fitzpatrick, who was a year behind me in school. We both qualified to participate in the State Track and Field Championships at Ohio State University, Columbus, Ohio.

In 1953, my senior year, I felt I was a sure bet to place second or third in the 220 at the State Track Championship Meet. My goal was to be in the State Record Book, and this was my last chance! Again I would likely be right behind John, who had the fastest time in the state and was a favorite to win. In the preliminary heats, one had to place first or second to make the finals. The heats were organized by one's best time in past meets. The six fastest runners were in the first heat, the next six were in the next heat, and so on.

To ensure one of us made the finals, Coach Quesinberry shuffled our positions and put me in the first, and fastest heat, and John in the second – the reverse of the way we had originally been assigned.

Coach informed me, "McCormick, I am going to switch heats with you and John to make sure we get a spot in the finals." With

Coach the team and the school always came first.

It was a statement, not a proposal nor a question. One just did not argue such decisions with Coach. Resigned to my situation, I recall thinking, *this has to be my best race ever, and to have a shot at the finals I must get a good start off the blocks.*

I was upset and nervous but determined. I took a few practice starts and ran twenty yards or so to warm up. The official starter ordered the ten fastest guys in the state to the starting line. He yelled, "Runners, on your marks!" Then after what seemed like a long delay he shouted, "Set!"

I rose up into my starting position. I planned to anticipate the starting gun rather than wait for it – a risky process in which you can be disqualified if you leave early. *I counted one thousand one, thousand two* then burst out of the blocks just as the starting gun fired. A great start! I was neck and neck with the leader. Two hundred twenty yards later the first three of us crossed the finish line very close together; but I knew I had not quite succeeded. I placed third; the second place finisher beat me by a whisker. I did not get to run in the finals.

Assistant Coach Lopatt was at the finish line. He immediately came over to me and said, "Great race, Ron. I timed you and that was a personal best time for you." He added, "I am very sorry you did not qualify for the finals".

There was a final set of ironies to this story. John was leading his heat by a comfortable margin but pulled up short of the finish line, mistaking another white line across the track as the finish. The rest of the runners blew by him, so he did not get to run in the finals either.

The runner that placed third in the state 220-yard finals was a fellow from another small high school in our district. Earlier that spring, as we had lined up at the starting line in the district meet, he had given me a haughty look and a derisive smile. I beat him decisively at that qualifying meet. His name made the record books as placing in the Track and Field Championship meet in the State of Ohio in 1953.

This time it just did not work out. I forgive you, Coach.

Later in his career Coach Quesinberry was selected as the National Athletic Director of the Year, a well deserved honor. His name is enshrined in several Athletic Halls of Fame in the State of Ohio. More importantly, with his statewide connections and influence he helped many students achieve their career ambition to attend college or be selected for a military academy. Coach was an original.

Academics

For the record, I need to say I wasn't a complete dud as a scholar in high school. Yes, hunting, fishing and sports were high on my list of interesting things to do, and studying and homework were not. There were a few exceptions, and at least one of note.

Mrs. Edna Gifford was my fifth grade teacher. She was a quiet, pleasant lady whose hobby was birds. She would interrupt the class when an interesting bird appeared in a tree outside the classroom windows. We would all rush to the window, and Mrs. Gifford would identify the bird and talk about its habits of feeding, nesting and rearing young. I always found this far more interesting than the Math or English we were studying. I looked forward to her unofficial lessons in ornithology.

A few students soon grew wise to the situation, and when the class was boring and time dragging, one would call attention to a bird outside, real or imagined. It provided a convenient diversion. The teacher was nicknamed 'Birdie' Gifford by the students.

On occasional Saturday mornings in the spring Mrs. Gifford would organize and lead a field trip to a marshy area along the 'Pipe'. The spring rituals of wetland and other birds were in full swing, and the area was alive with birdcalls and songs. The red-winged blackbirds were particularly active and flamboyant with their sleek, black bodies and bright red and yellow wing patches.

I enjoyed these 'birding trips' a great deal and remain indebted to a good teacher, Mrs. Gifford.

Ms. Elsa Jane Carroll was my high school English teacher and homeroom teacher. She was a dramatic and forceful teacher who was revered by her students and was a legend in her own right. Homework assignments often involved preparing essays. She was aware of my interest in the outdoors, and following class one day she took me aside. She challenged me to describe in an essay what fascinated me so about the woodlands and fields of our Chagrin River Valley. I labored over a two-page essay on my experiences squirrel hunting in the fall, and the splendor of our hardwood forests of northern Ohio. I kept that essay, marked up with her distinctive green ink, which ended with yet another challenge: "I dare you to keep this up – that is the ability to express yourself so clearly and effectively."

Through her challenge, encouragement and coaching, I discovered that I could write and even enjoyed it. Her lesson and my discovery paid great dividends over the course of my college education and Forest Service career.

I graduated from high school in 1953 without distinction but applied for and was accepted into the Ohio State University in Columbus, Ohio.

Mom and Dad. Frances and 'Mack' McCormick

Front porch on Bradley Street, Chagrin Falls, Ohio

Some of the neighborhood gang

First lesson on how to set a trap.

C. Bruce Crittenden

Bruce Crittenden, expert trapper

39

Jerry, Mack (Dad) and Ron

aug. 13, 1946

CLEVELAND NEWS

Chagrin Valley Circus Scores a Huge Hit—and Rings Up Milk Fund Cash

Animal trainers Peter Southmayd and Billy Rowe

Clowns amuse audience

It's always circus time in the Chagrin Valley—and the Bradley Street Performers are having as much fun as the audiences attending their shows.

Back yards on Bradley St. have been transformed into dressing rooms, a menagerie and an outdoor stage. The customers (admission is three cents) are content to sit on planks, in wheelbarrows or on the grass.

A dress parade down Main St. with Ringmaster Ronald McCormick leading the child performers, attracted a crowd of 103 for the first show.

First act of the afternoon, a dancing skit, was Gale Crittenden, 147 Bradley St., and Jerry McCormick, 171 Bradley St. They were given a grand introduction in true circus style by Ringmaster Ronald.

Early arrivals got choice seats. Barbara Myers, 154 Bradley St., held

Paul Rowe, 151 Bradley St., while he watched his first circus. Mrs. Frances McCormick, 171 Bradley St., Patty Stoneman, 58 Philomethian Ave., Claire Crittenden, 147 Bradley St., Mrs. William Rowe, 151 Bradley St., Barbara Brown, Bellevue Ave., and Robert Hartman, 119 S. Main St. voted the clown the funniest they have ever seen.

Dogs Take Lions' Role

Peter Southmayd, 157 Bradley St., and Billy Rowe, 151 Bradley St., were dressed as animal trainers and convinced the crowd that their dogs were ferocious lions.

The days profits of $3.60 (lemonade and pop corn), was sent to the Greater Cleveland Milk Fund for Underprivileged Children and the Bradley St. performers ended a tired but happy day.

And, any time, they'll put the big show on again—weather (and paying customers) permitting.

Gale Crittenden and Jerry McCormick, midgets, listen to Ringmaster Ronald McCormick

The famous Bradley Street Circus

CHAPTER THREE

Preparation

My application to attend Ohio State University was accepted, in spite of my mediocre high school academic record.

In the fall of 1953, Mom and Dad drove me the 150 miles to Columbus, Ohio, the home of OSU. The mission was to find me a place to live. Thousands of parents across the country were doing the same thing full of both hope and trepidation.

We located a third-floor flat (a converted attic) that I would share with three other freshman boys. It worked out fine. My bed was a small cot that just fit in the space created by a bay window. Nearby was an old, white enamel kitchen table I used for a desk. Not a particularly inspiring way to start college, but the rent was cheap!

The OSU campus was huge, and I was lost most of the time that first week looking for the buildings that offered my classes. I figured out early that the plain, depressing flat was not a place I could study or do homework – no inspiration and too many distractions. I walked to the Student Union or the campus library after dinner to study until about ten, and then I went home to bed. I lived a Spartan existence.

I was determined to do well. I felt I had something to prove. Late in my senior year, I had engaged in a career counseling session with High School Principal Ted Gurney. Mom accompanied me and informed Mr. Gurney I was interested in going to OSU. He looked surprised, then turned to her and said, "Mrs. McCormick, Ronald is a nice boy, but his academic record doesn't suggest he is college material. I recommend that your son pursue a trade." He proceeded to talk about several trade options.

I saw Mom's back stiffen and those prominent Pinter jaws tighten. I could tell she was not pleased. She responded, "Well, I guess we will just see about that." And we left.

I thought Mr. Gurney's judgment was premature, and I was embarrassed and angered. I was determined to do well at OSU and make sure Principal Gurney was kept informed. It is interesting how simple events alter the direction of a person's life. The previous summer Mom had arranged for me to spend a couple of days with a forester in Southern Ohio. The two events provided a goal and the incentive; both had been missing in me. In a larger sense it resulted in providing meaning to the rest of my life. Thanks Mr. Gurney. And a special thanks to you, Mom!

Principal Gurney was correct in that I had a lot of catch-up to do. Among my first quarter courses I took remedial Math – students called it 'bonehead' Math – and a very basic English course. I worked hard.

I recently discovered that Mom had saved the statements of grades from the OSU Registrar's Office. They had been squirreled away for fifty years. Looking at them brought back memories of both struggle and success. That first quarter I received an A in Physical Ed., an A in basic Agriculture, a C in Air Science (ROTC), a B in Botany – that one was important to me, I liked Botany – then a C in English and a C in Math. That was a 2.5 grade point average and good enough to start another quarter! I made sure a copy was sent to Principal Gurney at Chagrin Falls High School.

I joined a fraternity, Beta Theta Pi. Bruce Crittenden's dad had been a Beta at Ohio Wesleyan and encouraged Bruce to attend that college twenty-five miles or so down the highway from Columbus and Ohio State. Bruce pledged Beta there. His dad wrote a letter of referral for me to the Beta chapter at OSU. So Bruce and I both became Betas – fraternity brothers. I often ate dinner at the Beta

House, and I was required to wear a coat and tie to do so. I participated in the singing of traditional fraternity songs before and after dinner and particularly enjoyed that aspect of fraternity life.

There was one stark reminder of how things could go in the first year of college. One of my roommates flunked out following the first quarter and left Ohio State. That got my attention.

I did a little better the next quarter and each quarter after that. I had proved to myself that with hard work I could do well in college.

An Idaho Adventure

In the spring quarter of my freshman year, 1954, I took a class called 'Introduction to Forestry'. It was my first forestry class. I noticed a flyer on the bulletin board outside of the classroom. The Clearwater National Forest in Idaho was hiring for positions on a brush-cutting crew. I had no idea where the Clearwater Forest was located and, for that matter, no more than a vague notion about Idaho and the Forest Service. I checked an atlas and found that the forest was located in the panhandle of northern Idaho. That sounded good to me, so I sent in an application and was hired!

In early June I traveled west with a classmate from OSU who had taken a similar job on another national forest in Idaho. He had an old car, so we drove west. That was my first trip west of the Mississippi River, and it was an eye opener! I had only seen mountains, plains and rivers like that in western movies.

We drove through the Big Horn Mountains of Wyoming on a brilliantly clear, full moon night. The scenes I watched through the windshield reminded me of good black and white photographs – absent color, but starkly clear and sharp. Coming around a turn, we encountered a large herd of elk grazing in a meadow just below the highway. I had never seen an elk, much less an entire herd in a mountain meadow bathed in moonlight. The huge animals appeared majestically surreal. The moment was magical, and I knew I would really like the Western United States.

My classmate, a fellow from Wooster, Ohio, dropped me off at the Musselshell Ranger Station, an hour's drive outside of Pierce, Idaho. Pierce itself was a tiny town with a graveled main street through its center and weathered, clapboard buildings on each side. Just like those western movies.

I was assigned a cot in the barracks at Musselshell. Following some orientation and training, I spent the summer with a twenty-man crew cutting and piling roadside brush (called 'slash' in woods-speak) that had been generated by a logging contractor building access roads into the magnificent, white pine forest that was the Clearwater. We cut and piled brush all day, day after day. I became very proficient at wielding a double bit ax and keeping the business ends very sharp.

The man who supervised the work camp at Musselshell liked softball. He organized our crew into a team, and on Saturdays he would haul us in the back of the stake-side truck to Pierce to play other local teams. We did not have much time to practice, and we weren't very good.

It was, however, a nice diversion and an opportunity to get out of the camp for a change of scene. We wouldn't return until late evening, which gave us a chance to walk around the little town. Pierce had one old hotel that also offered a bar; it was the local hangout for loggers.

One Saturday evening I noticed a line of men standing outside of the hotel. It was a line of loggers dressed in black, stagged-off *Can't Bust 'Em* pants, course wool shirts and suspenders. The line of rugged-looking loggers crossed the sagging, wooden porch and spilled into the dusty street.

I asked our supervisor, "What's that line all about? What are they selling in there?"

He smiled at me patiently and said, "Ron, why don't you get in line behind Buck and find out?"

Buck was a big, broad-shouldered man of about thirty, and the straw boss or second-in-command of our crew. I stepped in behind him and asked, "What's going on Buck, what's the line for?"

He looked at me with derision and said, "Flossie – we're waiting for a crack at Flossie. She's here tonight and the only one in town."

I felt my face turn warm and very red I am sure, and I bolted from the line. The men in line had been watching and enjoyed a good laugh. Boy, I was sure an innocent, naïve kid from Chagrin Falls!

I needed to leave for home in early September to get ready for another year of college. I had been sending most of my earnings home for Mom to deposit in my bank account, designated for college tuition and books. I had about fifteen dollars for travel expenses, so I decided to hitchhike home. Frugality was only part of the reason; I wanted to turn the trip into an experience – another adventure!

In the 1950s, hitchhiking was more common than today and relatively safe. Hitching south toward Boise, Idaho, on my fourth or fifth ride I was picked up by a steelworker from Spokane, Washington. He was a swarthy, short but powerfully built man who promptly began to tell me his story. He occasionally paused to take swigs from a bottle in a brown paper bag that rested on the seat between us. He offered me a drink, but I declined. At that point in my life I didn't drink, smoke, or stand in lines outside old hotels. Not to suggest I do now!

The steelworker told me he had been a professional boxer but had to quit because of repeated broken bones in his hands. He said he was a good fighter, a highly ranked middleweight. He bragged about fighting (and losing) to Tony Zale, who sometime later fought Rocky Graziano for the middleweight championship of the world. I recalled the Graziano-Zale match, I had listened to it on the radio a few years earlier, and it was a typical, punishing,

Graziano-style battle. Graziano won.

The steelworker told me about his girlfriend, a cocktail waitress in a tavern in Boise.

"The slimy bartender in that dumpy joint is making moves on my girlfriend, and I'm going down there to whip his butt, and anyone else in the bar that has similar ideas."

"I could use some help, why don't you join me and we'll clean out the place?"

I was startled, and a vision of a bloody bar fight, arrest and a night in the Boise jail filled by head.

Well, in those days I thought I was pretty tough, but I wasn't dumb. "I just can't do that. I must get back to Ohio so I can go back to college," I mumbled.

He just laughed and said OK. "But you're going to miss out on a good time!"

I have always wondered how that episode of his life turned out, and what might have happened if I had gone along with him. He dropped me off on the edge of town, and I spent two of my fifteen-dollar travel budget to stay the night in a cheap Boise hotel (flop house). The little room didn't have a door and noises in the hallway kept me awake and a bit anxious. I didn't get much sleep.

In an ensuing ride, I was searched by an encyclopedia salesman as a condition of riding with him. He had been previously robbed at knifepoint, he wanted to take a look in my little gym bag, which only contained a couple of changes of clothes.

On another ride a rancher dropped me off at a dirt road intersection on highway 66 in the middle of nowhere, saying, "Here is where I turn, son." Cars were flying by in both directions. It took me forever to catch another ride east.

I slept outside all but that one night in Boise. I recall making a bed in a utility trailer stored in a backyard. It had a tarp thrown over it, and I just crawled under the tarp. The trailer was propped up at an angle, and I spent an uncomfortable night. When I was lucky, I would get a ride with someone that was traveling overnight.

It was raining hard when I arrived in Cheyenne, Wyoming, so I went to a matinee movie to wait out the storm. The movie was *The Student Prince* with tenor Mario Lanza. Whenever I recall that event I remember his rousing rendition of *Drink, Drink, Drink*. Lanza was known as the 'Voice of the Century'. He died in 1959 at age thirty-eight of a heart attack.

Finally, after more than two hundred rides – I counted them – and four and a half days, I arrived at 171 Bradley Street, Chagrin Falls, Ohio. Home!

On the last ride the driver felt sorry for me and delivered me right to my front door. I had a memorable adventure and two dollars left in my wallet!

Cleveland Metropolitan Parks

The summer following high school graduation I was employed by the local headquarters for the Cleveland Metropolitan Park system. The parks were a necklace of hardwood forests and rivers that draped around the gritty, hardworking city of Cleveland. They were a great public asset and heavily used by the Cleveland residents.

The local superintendent was the father of Johnny Hurst, a neighborhood friend who was a year ahead of me in high school. Mr. Hurst hired his son and other local high school boys as laborers for campground cleanup, maintenance, and road repairs.

Following my sophomore year at OSU, I decided to stay home and work another summer for the park. It was good, practical outdoor work experience and an on-the-ground education in park and campground management and maintenance. In addition, I could save more money for college by living at home. It was, however, my last summer at home in Chagrin Falls.

University of Michigan

At the time, Ohio State only offered a two-year curriculum towards a degree in Forest Management. At the conclusion of the two years, I needed to transfer to a college or university that offered a four-year program and a Bachelor of Science Degree in Forestry.

I decided to attend the University of Michigan. I chose it because it had an outstanding reputation for the quality of its School of Natural Resources, and because it was within a day's drive of Chagrin Falls. However, I believe I mostly chose it because my girlfriend, Shirley Curtis, with whom I had been 'going steady' since our junior year in high school, was transferring to Michigan from Ohio Wesleyan. I applied and was grateful, even a little surprised, to be accepted. My grades at OSU were apparently good enough to get into this prestigious university.

In the fall of 1955, Mom and Dad drove me to Ann Arbor, Michigan to search for housing. The first year I roomed with three guys in yet another third-floor attic apartment. One roommate stuttered and one stammered, especially when they were excited or arguing. They were both really nice guys, but it was hilarious to watch and listen to them in an argument. They were good-natured about it and also seemed to see the humor in their situation.

I was doing OK academically that fall at the U of M and surviving financially by receiving lunch and dinners in exchange for doing dishes at a local sorority house. I settled into a routine. Shirley and I seemed to be operating in different social circles, however. I was part of the blue-jean, plaid-shirt crowd who attended forestry classes at the university's School of Natural Resources, and she was one of the nicely dressed members of a large sorority. We still dated occasionally, but we were drifting apart.

Eventually we decided to call it quits. As the song goes, *'breaking up is hard to do,'* and it affected me more than I thought

49

it would. I felt a bit disoriented and lost focus on why I was going to college.

The Christmas Blues

I went home to Chagrin Falls for Christmas, as it was between semesters and I had some time. I hung out with some of my high school classmates, some of whom were also home from college for the Christmas break. We drank a little beer and talked about the mysteries of life.

The notion of joining the Marine Corps entered my head. Dad's brother, Jack, had been a Marine and often talked about his experiences in the Corps, mostly to other adults. I was a child but had listened in and absorbed the stories; they had made an impression on me. Besides, I liked and sought adventure and had this self-image of being tough enough to deal with any challenge, particularly a physical challenge. The idea grew more appealing to me, and it didn't occur to me at the time that I was running away.

A schoolmate and friend, George Plazak, was also hanging around town with no particular focus, and I talked to him about joining the Corps together. He was less enthusiastic than I, but he eventually agreed. Much to the dismay of his parents and mine, we signed up and boarded a train full of recruits bound for Parris Island, South Carolina.

We arrived in the late afternoon and were bussed from the train station to the notorious Parris Island Marine Corps Boot Camp. It was early February 1956. As the name suggests, it was located on a small island just off the coast, connected to the mainland by a causeway. It has been a USMC recruit training center since 1915.

George and I were assembled into a group with recruits off the same train, and we became Platoon 65 of "A" Company, 3rd Recruit Training Battalion.

The first twenty-four hours resembled boot camp as it is portrayed in the movies, only more so. We were insulted and harassed, made to stand at attention for long periods, had our heads shaved bald, issued training fatigues, and assigned to a barracks.

We were finally allowed to crawl into our bunks, and it must have been well after midnight. Our watches had been collected earlier, so no one knew the time. What seemed like only minutes later, the lights snapped back on, and a great clatter arose from the center of the squad bay. It was Drill Instructor (DI) Sgt. Barrose beating a metal trashcan with his heavy-duty swagger stick.

He shouted, "Get up, you lazy skinhead maggots! The last one to stand at attention in front of his rack will be beaten severely about the head and shoulders!" We believed him, and there was a furious scramble.

Sgt. Barrose was a short, stocky DI with a deeply tanned face and a neatly trimmed black mustache adorning his upper lip; his uniform pants and shirt were always freshly pressed. He carried a swagger stick, as did most DIs, but his appeared to be a sawed-off broomstick weighted on one end and painted black. He liked to rap recruits on the head, elbow or shoulder with it and did – frequently. There was a great deal of physical abuse, punching, slapping and hitting, usually when a recruit messed up, but sometimes just at random. This was before recruit-training reforms were instituted in late 1956 and early 1957.

When we were finally standing at attention, barefoot and shivering in our 'skivvies', Sgt. Barrose paraded down the center of the passageway of the barracks. He resembled a recruiting poster in crisply ironed trousers, military-creased shirt, wide-brimmed hat and swagger stick tucked under one arm. Ramrod straight, he stopped, turned and starred at each one of us. We were tired, disheveled-looking and wide-eyed scared. He would frown, shake his head, and move on to the next frightened and bewildered kid.

"Tomorrow morning," he bellowed, "when you hear my footsteps in the hallway, you had better be up. When I open the squad bay doors, I want to see seventy-five ugly, skinhead recruits standing at attention with a bed sheet under each arm and a pillowcase clamped in your yellow teeth!" (Expletives deleted.)

We were aghast. That meant we would have to listen for his approach. How could we sleep?

Marine Corps boot camp was a significant event for me. It was physically tough but mentally even more challenging. The objective seemed to be to break down a recruit both physically and mentally and build a Marine, all in twelve weeks. This was the peacetime Marine Corps just following the Korean War but before Vietnam. There seemed to be a bottled-up frustration in the DIs. I guessed that during peacetime promotions came slow, and most career marines seemed to long for the next war. That frustration was focused on the recruits.

There was also a strange, sometimes sadistic humor that accompanied the harassment and training, and I had never heard nor imagined such foul language. Cuss words were strung together and combined in the most imaginative ways, and new words and phrases were coined. Every once in a while I would catch George's eye, and we would both smile.

I soon realized that there was a competition among DIs, and they were evaluated on how well their training platoon did in marching drills, obstacle courses, and the rifle range. Thus they sought to weed out poor performers.

Across the passageway from my bunk, or 'rack' as they were called, was an overweight, clumsy kid who wore glasses and seemed way out of his element. The guy did poorly in marching drills, exercises and just about everything else. DI Barrose picked on him unmercifully. One evening Barrose entered the barracks, and we all scrambled rigidly to attention. He went over to the kid, grabbed his footlocker, and holding it chest high spilled the entire contents – clothes and personal gear – on the deck.

"Private," Sgt. Barrose announced in mock seriousness, "I am building you a boat." We watched, fascinated. He proceeded to get a mop out of a nearby bucket and placed it upright in the center of the footlocker, securing it with a piece of rope. He then jerked a sheet off the kid's bed and draped it over the mop handle.

"There," he said. "You now have a nice sailboat." He walked around it and admired his work. "I expect you to sail this across the channel to the mainland tonight, never to return."

He turned to leave, then added, "That channel is filled with sharks, and they love fat recruits, don't fall in!" With that he left, and we all remained at attention with mouths open. *Surely he is not serious.*

I looked at the kid across the passageway, and he had paled and was shaking. It was evident *he* thought Barrose was serious.

At dawn the next morning the kid was gone. He did not take the boat. I supposed he tried to somehow make the mainland and then home. In going AWOL, or Absent without Leave, he was sure to end up in the Marine Corps brig – a problem solved for the DI. A rumor persisted that on the mainland city of Beaufort, city police officers would receive a 'bounty' of fifty dollars for apprehending and returning a runner. We never saw the kid again.

Midway through the training we were scheduled to go to the rifle range for a week of instruction and practice firing the Garand M1 rifle. My old *Guidebook for Marines* describes the rifle as "a gas-operated, clip-fed, air-cooled, semiautomatic shoulder weapon." John Garand invented this rifle in 1924, and it was the standard weapon issued in World War II and the Korean War. It had an aperture rear sight, fired a 30-06 cartridge, and weighed 9.5 pounds. The serial number of my rifle was 4377070, which I committed to memory in 1956. The M1 rifle is now legend and has a dedicated website on the Internet, which opens with a rifle shot followed by the distinctive metallic ring of the clip being ejected.

I was looking forward to the rifle range, confident I would do well. All platoons were on a training schedule, and one platoon followed the other in the order they arrived on the Island.

The rifle range was a break in the routine. We moved to another barracks associated with the range, and for two weeks concentrated on learning the firing positions, bullet ballistics, adjustments for windage, etc. Marching was suspended and discipline more relaxed. The M1 was a very accurate rifle when sighted in and fired properly. I did very well, firing consistent scores of 220 to 235 out of a possible 250. That put me in the 'Expert' classification, and the drill instructors were pleased. I could sense a higher level of respect from them, although the actual treatment didn't change much.

A week or so following the rifle range we were back in our original barracks. Late one night Sgt. Barrose charged into the squad bay. He was wet, muddy and appeared agitated. It was Sunday night, April 8, 1956.

We jerked awake and clamored out of our racks. He stood us at attention and blared, "We drowned seven of you skinhead maggots tonight, and if this platoon doesn't shape up, we will drown seven more tomorrow!" He glared at us for a moment longer, then turned out the lights and abruptly left, leaving us standing at attention in the dark, wondering what in the world was going on. I had an impression he had been drinking, as he was not his usual nattily attired, composed self.

We were never told the whole story, but by piecing together tidbits of rumor, or 'scuttlebutt', we learned that a platoon following behind us in the training schedule, and a couple of days from completing the rifle range, had been ordered by their DI to do a nighttime forced march. He had led them through the tidal swamps that lined the seaward side of the island and into an estuary called Ribbon Creek. Apparently there was an incoming tide. The scuttlebutt was that seven recruits had drowned. It was also whispered that their DI had been drinking.

Recently, wanting to tie down the facts about this event, I researched it on the Internet. There are volumes of information available, and even a book documenting the event and the trial of the platoon's drill instructor. One of the most compelling pieces I found was a description by Gene Ervin, as published on the Marines' Globe and Anchor Internet forum. Mr. Ervin was a member of the ill-fated Platoon 71 that was marched into Ribbon Creek that night.

Mr. Ervin reported that their DI, Sgt. Mat McKeon, became embarrassed and angry when it was reported to him that members of his platoon were 'goofing off' while doing their laundry in the back of the barracks. Matters were made even worse later that evening when some of these same recruits had the audacity to go for seconds in the chow line.

In order to reestablish discipline, McKeon ordered a complete 'hands and knees' scrub down of the barracks. ("All I want to see is elbows and assholes," Sgt. Barrose would say.) Then, as it was getting dark, he ordered the platoon to fall in outside for a night march. He marched them into the center of Ribbon Creek, and by that time it was very dark. There was disorientation and confusion, and the incoming tidal current lifted some of the recruits off their feet. Many of them could not swim. Most of the platoon made it back to the bank, and Sgt. McKeon led them back to the barracks. Then he called for a count off; they were short seven recruits.

It wasn't till morning that six bodies were located in Ribbon Creek. The seventh missing recruit had made it across the creek and kept on going, headed for his home in North Carolina.

This became a front-page story nationally, but I was only vaguely aware of the furor at the time. We did not have access to radios or newspapers. Sgt. McKeon was placed in the brig and later court-martialed. He was convicted of negligent homicide and drinking on duty and sentenced to nine months confinement at hard labor and a bad conduct discharge. Upon review by the Secretary of the Navy, the sentence was reduced to three months and the discharge set aside.

As a result of this tragic night march, the entire training program of the Marine Corps was torn apart and restructured, and a modicum of humanity and common sense inserted into the new program. The period before the Ribbon Creek incident is now referred to as 'the old Marine Corps' – with a hint of pride emanating from Marines of that era.

I have a lot more boot camp stories I could tell, but you get the idea, and I need to move on. I remember my rifle serial number and personal ID number to this day, emblazoned on my memory by fear I suppose. Yet, all in all, I have a positive feeling about the Marine Corps Boot Camp experience. I learned a lot about myself.

Toward the end of boot camp I had developed a rash on the inside of my fingers of both hands. In the dirt and grime of the rifle range my fingers became infected. I tried to hide the fact from the DIs, as I really wanted to finish boot camp and graduate with my platoon. I did not want to be set back while waiting for my hands to heal. I would then be assigned to a new platoon.

A couple of weeks before we were to graduate from boot camp, we were standing at attention on the parade grounds, rifles at port arms for a rifle inspection. Sgt. Barrose stood in front of me and was about to snatch the rifle away for inspection when he noticed my fingers bleeding and oozing pus.

"What is that crud on your fingers, recruit?"

"Just a little infection, sir," I replied.

He looked closely at my hands, frowned, and ordered me to report to sickbay.

A navy corpsman in sickbay treated and bandaged my fingers, and I returned to the platoon. However, my fingers did not get better. One morning Sgt. Barrose came in the barracks and said I had been ordered to report to the Naval Hospital in Charleston, S.C. He added, and I will never forget it, "Why is it just the good ones get taken away?" It was the closest to a compliment I ever heard from him.

After a couple of weeks in the hospital they got the infection under control, and the fingers began to heal. They concluded the rash and irritation was caused by an allergy of some sort, perhaps due to the rifle cleaning and oiling substances, but they couldn't pin down the cause.

One morning I was ordered to report to the officer in charge of the hospital. Upon entering his office, a navy captain was studying my personnel file.

"Take a seat, Private McCormick," he said, glancing up as he read the file.

I sat down. He looked up and said, rather informally I thought, "I see you were attending the University of Michigan when you enlisted."

"Yes, sir," I replied. "I was studying for a degree in Forest Management."

He looked at me thoughtfully, and then said, "I am going to make this short. You have two choices, I can discharge you from the hospital and send you back to Parris Island, where you would be assigned to a new platoon, and you can complete your training." He paused, looking intently at me. "Or," he went on, "I can recommend you for an honorable discharge if you will agree to return to college. You have until tomorrow morning to decide. That will be all."

My head was swimming. I did want to complete boot camp and become a full-fledged Marine and finish my two-year enlistment. But I would not be able to go back and graduate with my original platoon and my friend, George. I would be in a new platoon.

I knew there might be a possibility I could get back to Michigan in time to attend the Forestry Summer Camp in the Upper Peninsula. The summer camp, designed for field training in surveying, mapping, and timber cruising, was a requirement for graduation, and I could catch up with my classmates there as well.

I called Mom that evening and asked her to call the U of M School of Natural Resources to see if I could get registered for the summer camp. She made a few calls and was told they would save a spot for me. The next morning I called Mom and she gave me the good news.

I reported to the navy captain, stood at attention in front of his desk, and told him I was enrolled to return to the U of M that summer.

He glanced up at me, smiled and said, "Good decision, Private McCormick."

This wise officer was looking at the big picture and my future, and he very likely influenced the course of my life. He followed through and I received an honorable discharge on 31 May, 1956. The experience at Parris Island remains vivid in my memory, and I am proud of my deportment there under the demanding training conditions of 1956 in the 'Old Marine Corps'.

Return to Michigan

Camp Filibert Roth, the site of the U of M Forestry Summer Camp, was located on Michigan's rural and remote Upper Peninsula. It was situated on the shores of Golden Lake within the Ottawa National Forest. This was a picturesque north-woods setting of hardwood forests, bogs and lakes. The call of the loons in the evening completed the idyllic scene.

I was assigned to room with Dave Lanham, John Chansler, Dave Clements and Ben Monahan in a small, rustic cabin. We completed field exercises as a team and studied together. Ben had a car, and on Friday nights we traveled to the nearby mining town of Iron River. The residents worked the open pit iron ore mines. We drank beer and danced with the local girls to the music of local Polka bands.

At the end of summer I returned to Chagrin Falls for a brief respite before resuming classes at the U of M. I decided I wanted a car to drive back to Michigan. Dad had located an early-fifties model Studebaker for me. I drove it back to Ann Arbor and enrolled for the fall term.

The following spring, during spring break, a roommate and two other friends and I loaded up the old Studebaker and drove straight through to the Florida Keys intent on scuba diving. The little car was overloaded with people, diving gear and air tanks. The floorboards in the car were rusting out and sagged with all the weight. I saw daylight between the floorboards and the doors and felt the cold Michigan air rushing in!

One of my roommates, a fisheries biology student, had taken a course in scuba diving as part of his curriculum. In the evenings at the university pool, he gave us a short course on the basics of using scuba gear. By today's standards we were woefully unprepared for deep water diving and ignorant of the risks of diving – risks that are now emphasized in a required certification course.

We made it to Marathon Key in seventeen hours of continuous driving. We were on a bare-bones budget and leased a cheap motel room for a week. We rented a boat and outboard motor each day and headed out to a reef just off Alligator Lighthouse. We did this long before the sport was popular, and we had the reef to ourselves. The water was warm, amazingly clear, and teeming with fish and marine life. I was hooked and continued to scuba dive for many years. I did eventually get properly certified.

A Second Trip West

At the conclusion of my junior year at the U of M, I applied and was accepted for a summer job on a survey crew on the Stanislaus National Forest out of Sonora, California. An acquaintance in the School of Natural Resources, Steve Harper, had also secured a summer job out west, so we made the trip together in his car.

I was assigned to a five-person survey crew, and we located and staked roads for access to future timber sales. I really liked central California and the Sierra Nevada – great climate, beautiful mountains, and more young ladies to date on weekends. This was in contrast to northern Idaho, which seemed to have a deficit of young women. I think they left those small, remote towns as soon as they came of age.

For the fall return trip, I had arranged with Steve to meet him in Reno, Nevada at the downtown bus station on a specified date and time. I took the Greyhound bus from Sonora to Reno. My days of hitchhiking home across the United States were over.

I had the good fortune to choose a seat next to a plump, but attractive, dark-haired young lady. She smiled at me as I sat down, and we engaged in a conversation about our young lives, and what we had been doing that summer. It was a long bus ride, up and over the Sierra Nevada Mountains then down into Nevada, stopping for lunch along the way. We had lunch together, and on returning to the bus we chose a seat in the very back row. We liked each other and 'made out' for most of the trip to Reno.

An older, gray-haired woman a few seats forward kept looking back at us and scowling. I could see the bus driver watching us in the rear-view mirror. I thought I saw him smile, so I didn't worry about getting evicted. By today's standards our amorous activities were quite innocent. When we arrived at the Reno bus station, her parents were waiting for her, and she asked me to meet them. I begged off, making the excuse I had to find Steve, who was supposed to be there. She was disappointed, but we hugged, wished each other a good life, and parted company. I had to get home and back to college. I located Steve, and we headed east.

Graduation

During the summer camp at Filibert Roth, Dave, Jack, John and I found we were compatible roommates and decided to room together in Ann Arbor for our final year at the U of M. We rented a basement apartment and fell into a routine of going to class, studying, and drinking beer on Friday nights at the Pretzel Bell, the local campus watering hole.

Talking over a beer one night, Dave Lanham and I discovered we had both trapped muskrats as teenagers, and we still had our traps. We agreed to run a joint trap line that fall. We figured we could make enough for pocket money and help finance our incidental expenses. I drove home one weekend to pick up my old traps, and then returned to Ann Arbor.

We were both skilled in locating muskrat habitat and making good sets. We caught a good number of muskrats, a few raccoons and even a mink.

Space was limited in the small apartment. We placed our fur pelts, skin side out, on drying boards and hung them from the closet pole in the entryway closet. One Friday evening my three roommates and I had dates with nursing school students.

Wanting to do something different and impress these four young ladies, we invited them over for a fried raccoon dinner. The unfortunate raccoon had blundered into one of our muskrat traps, and when that happened, as it occasionally did, we would harvest it for food. Actually, seasoned and floured, fried raccoon makes a tasty main course, especially for four always-hungry forestry students.

We had planned to just drape their coats over the furniture, but one of the ladies decided she wanted to hang up her new coat instead, and before we could react she opened the entry hall closet door and gasped.

An ugly scene befitting a horror movie confronted her, and a strange odor wafted into the room. The young lady paled, her hand instinctively finding her throat as she screamed.

The girls reluctantly stayed for dinner, picking at their fried raccoon. They made a lame excuse and left soon after. We never saw them again, but I know they had a story to tell their friends about the strange forestry students who kept animal skins in their apartment and feasted on dead critters.

Other than a few side attractions, I worked hard at the University of Michigan and did well academically. I graduated in June 1983 with over a 3.0 or B average my final year of college.

A Forester's Lament

In 1903 the Department of Forestry was created at the University of Michigan and chaired by Filibert Roth until 1923. This department eventually evolved into the School of Natural Resources.

It is, of course, essential and fitting that a dynamic university keeps up with the times and tailors their programs accordingly. In 1982 the U of M School of Natural Resources was renamed the School of Natural Resources and Environment. The four-year program leading to a Bachelor of Science Degree in Forestry was not long ago phased out in favor of a Master of Science Degree in Terrestrial Ecosystems. Timely courses such as ecology and conflict resolution are now offered.

In 1988 Camp Filibert Roth was decommissioned and field training moved to the university's biological station at Douglas Lake, near the campus.

I could not find the term 'forester' mentioned on the School of Natural Resources and Environment website. It seems the name of my once-proud profession had migrated to car lots and to a nameplate on a vehicle.

Thus 'forester' has become historical lore, emblematic of a bygone era. It has gone the way of Indian, Apache, Comanche, Ranger and others. Some of the best-known, romantic legends and symbols of our history are now found as names and images suitable for cars and sports teams.

I understand that universities and professions and organizations must continually re-invent themselves to stay relevant in a swiftly moving world, but it saddens me to realize that in the short duration of a career, my professional identity became an anachronism.

University of Michigan Forestry Summer Camp, 1956

CHAPTER FOUR

The Calling

D ave Scott, a good friend and former boss, once said that a career with the Forest Service was more than a job, it was a 'calling'. I believe he was correct. People of my era seemed to have been drawn to the organization for its mission and reputation, more than just a way to practice their chosen profession and earn a living.

This was an awakening of the spirit and a calling to a life's work. The dedication, accomplishments and camaraderie of the people of this era is now legend.

My career took the family and me to seven national forests in three states and one regional office. I always looked forward to the challenge and opportunity of a new assignment and relished the idea of experiencing a new national forest, its mountain ranges, forests and rivers. I knew this was where I wanted to be. It was what I wanted to do.

Stanislaus National Forest

I mentioned earlier that I worked the summer of 1957 on the Stanislaus National Forest in California working on a survey crew. Following graduation from the University of Michigan in June 1958, I accepted a job offer to return to the Stanislaus as a GS-5 engineering aid at a salary of $4,340 per annum. This was to be a temporary classification until they could obtain a formal appointment for me as a professional forester.

I had simultaneously received an offer from the Coconino National Forest out of Flagstaff, Arizona. It was to be a formal appointment as a forester from the start, and in that sense a better job offer than the Stanislaus offer. However, I liked the forest in California, and I already knew the people I would be working with, so I accepted their offer. I have often speculated on what direction my career and life would have taken if I had gone to the Coconino. No regrets, however.

I continued doing the forest road location and survey work similar to what I had done the previous summer, but I was assigned a three-person crew of temporary summer employees. I was suddenly a leader, a boss! That was my first exposure to supervision, and with no specific training – learn on the job. Our little survey crew camped out of town in a tent camp all week and would return to Sonora on Friday evening. Early Monday mornings before leaving town we would stop at a market to purchase our groceries and supplies for the week.

I would prepare a grocery list and assign one person to get breakfast items, one the dinners, and another to purchase sandwich makings and fruit for our sack lunches. When we reached camp I soon discovered the lunch items consisted of bread and several jars of 'sandwich spread' – basically mayonnaise with pickle pieces in it. The young man had likely never shopped for groceries before and didn't know any better. We lived on this 'spread' for lunches for a week, and I learned a lesson about clear instructions, delegation and follow-up.

The role and importance of the Forest Service was expanding, and so was the size of the workforce. There was an influx of young foresters just out of college. It was also a time when the leadership in the regional offices orchestrated all transfers and promotions. Several months into my career I felt forgotten as I watched my contemporaries promoted to GS-7 and transferred to other ranger districts on other national forests. I grew a bit impatient.

Several brand-new foresters, just out of college, were hired by the Stanislaus in 1957 and 1958. A few of them were to become lifelong friends; Erwin Ward was one of those. He was also from the east – New York State. Raised in a rural area of upstate New York, he graduated from the renowned forestry school at Syracuse University. Between college years he had also worked summers on western national forests.

As our careers progressed and we each followed our separate but similar career paths, Erwin and I lost touch. Then, in 2008 I received an e-mail from Erwin. He and his wife, Adela, were going to celebrate their fiftieth wedding anniversary in January 2009, and he wanted me to attend.

Erwin reminded me I had been a groomsman at their wedding in 1959 in Sonora, California. The memory of that wedding had faded in my memory. Erwin had also tracked down Dave Hudson, who had been another one of the young foresters recruited in that period. Dave had also been a groomsman.

The anniversary celebration was held in Santa Barbara, California. A two-day drive for us from Grants Pass, but Carol and I decided to attend; so did Dave. We were so glad we did. It was an enjoyable and touching celebration, and a pleasant reunion of old friends.

Back on the Stanislaus in 1959, Erwin and Dave had been promoted and moved on. I was still waiting. Six months or so later I finally received my full-time appointment and was officially a 'Junior Forester'. The title seemed to me to be a demeaning moniker – the 'junior' part. It was used informally at the time, particularly by 'old hands', to describe foresters just beginning their careers. Something like the term 'shave-tail lieutenants' as used in the military.

I had long admired the bronze badge pinned to the breast pocket of the shirts of permanent, full-time employees. It is a standard shield shape featuring a pine tree in its center bracketed by a large 'U' and 'S'. I wanted one. Shortly after receiving my permanent appointment I was given a badge, not by some high-ranking official in a solemn ceremony as I had imagined, but by a property clerk saying the badge was government property and telling me I must sign a form and return it if I quit or was transferred. Anyway, a co-worker instructed me to wear it on the flap of my uniform shirt pocket, over my heart. I did so with a large measure of pride.

I must confess here and now that when, years later, I received a district ranger assignment I vowed not to give up that particular badge. An understanding property clerk, through some magic, covered my tracks, and I have that badge to this day – a meaningful memento and symbol of a career.

My next assignment as a junior forester was to search for and mark with paint beetle-infected and dying ponderosa pine. The off-color tops and red 'flags' of the dying branches were the indicators. Once infested to that degree the trees would be dead within a year. Harvesting them now would slow the spread of the beetles. These trees would later be salvaged by a pair of 'gypo' loggers the forest had contracted. I was assigned a pickup truck and provided a paint gun to mark the trees.

I roamed the forest, designated trees for harvest, measured diameter and estimated the number of saw logs the tree contained, and noted the location on a map for the loggers. I would check on the loggers from time to time to ensure they cut up any slash they had created, and that they had installed erosion control water bars across the skid trails they had created while pulling logs to a landing. This was a very basic form of timber sale administration. It was up to me to get the job done correctly. Again, I was learning on the job. It was also a great way to learn the forest and its road system. It was real forestry work at last!

One day, while following a district employee driving down a very dusty road, my vision became obscured by flying dust, and I ran the pickup off the road and down an embankment. The truck rolled over once and stopped upright against a tree. There was quite a bit of damage to the truck, but I was not injured. The pickup was actually assigned to the forest timber staff officer, who had loaned it to me for the tree salvage task. He was very upset, and I subsequently received a disciplinary letter. The Forest Service always took safety very seriously. The event and aftermath frightened me, and I thought my career was over. It wasn't, but I had learned another valuable lesson.

Many national forests permit ranchers to graze cattle in the 'high country' during summer months. This activity is monitored closely, and animal numbers are determined by the calculated range 'carrying capacity'. One of the jobs of a young forester was to count cows being released onto the national forest range in the spring to ensure the numbers did not exceed the carrying capacity. The cattle were trucked up the mountain from private land pastures in the valley and released into a makeshift corral. On one such occasion I became acquainted with one of the cowboys, Bob McGowan. He was pushing the herd though the counting chute and I counted them as they exited the chute. Talking with him during a break, he mentioned that his girlfriend, Bonnie, had a friend from the Los Angeles area staying with her for the summer and that perhaps we could go out on a double date.

Sometime later he arranged the date, and I met and dated this young girl from the big city. She was an attractive, dark-haired, spirited young lady. Her name was Kaye Clark. We dated throughout the summer. That fall she moved to nearby Stockton to attend a school of cosmetology, and I drove down to Stockton on weekends to see her.

In the fall of 1959 I finally received my first promotion as GS-7 at a salary of $4,980 per annum. The following spring I was reassigned to the Calaveras Ranger District of the Stanislaus National Forest, headquartered in San Andreas, a small town in the foothills of the Sierra Nevada. On September 10, 1960 Kaye and I were married, and we rented a small apartment in town. My position was project sales officer, located far out of town in a place called Soap Creek, deep in a remote part of the forest. It proved to be both an interesting and challenging assignment.

Soap Creek was the location of a large logging camp operated by the Pickering Lumber Company. They operated a large sawmill about fifty miles away in Sonora. The camp was located around a railroad transfer landing. Huge off-road logging trucks hauled equally huge pine and fir logs out of the woods and offloaded there to have the logs loaded onto railroad cars for the trip down the mountain to the Pickering mill in Sonora. The engines were old Shay steam engines that ran day and night, switching cars around until a train was assembled. I didn't know it then, but I was witness to a bit of western logging history that was soon to give way to more modern transportation systems.

I lived in a boxcar-sized cabin that had been transported to the site by rail. It sat about fifty feet from the tracks. The old engine moved log cars all night which made it difficult to sleep. The cabin had a wood stove for heat and an outhouse for a bathroom. I ate breakfast and dinner in the cookhouse with about fifty loggers. Traditional logging camp rules were in effect, i.e. no talking in the cookhouse, eat your meal, pack a lunch and get out and go to work. The food was plain but good, and there was plenty of it.

I spent my weeks alternating between preparing the next year's timber sale (marking trees and designating road access) and administering the current sale operation for compliance with the terms of the timber sale contract. Sale administration mostly involved ensuring minimum stump heights, proper slash disposal, and that tractor skid trails were properly water-barred and closed to prevent erosion. Pickering was a good company to work with, and I did not have much trouble gaining contract compliance.

The forests of the Stanislaus were magnificent! Ponderosa and sugar pine four and five feet in diameter towered into the deep blue sky of the Sierra Nevada. Reddish barked incense cedar added color contrast, and the aroma emitted from their scaly leaves, mixed with the smells of the pine needles basking in the hot sun, was intoxicating. These were real forests. I felt fortunate and very happy to be there.

The new sale to be laid out and marked was beyond the end of the road. I used a topographic map and a compass for navigation. I would first locate and flag the general sale boundaries, encompassing about a thousand acres, then traverse across the area using a compass bearing so as not to get lost. I marked weak and high-risk trees for harvest and measured the diameter and height of twenty percent of them, randomly selected, in order to make an estimate of the total sale volume. That was an elemental form of a timber 'cruise', a basic task for a forester.

Sometimes I felt a twinge of regret when I squirted a bright blue slash of paint across the great trunk of one of these old trees. *But*, I rationalized, *I am carefully selecting and only marking those trees showing clear signs of declining health, or insect infestation or disease, and not likely to live another ten years.* In other words, harvesting the mortality. That was acceptable to me.

The forester for the Pickering Lumber Company would occasionally visit the sale I was preparing and always criticize me for marking 'too light' – that is, not enough trees. On their own lands, the company used what they termed an 'economic harvest'. Basically they cut anything over twenty-four inches in diameter. I had seen their harvest areas, and I didn't like the result.

I stuck with my own tree selection and marking system. It was consistent with what I had learned at the university and the bit of training I had received on the Stanislaus. My boss, Harry Schimke, had reviewed and approved what I was doing.

The new sale area I was preparing was unroaded, wild and uninhabited. Blundering onto rattlesnakes and black bears was a daily occurrence. Initially, being alone all day in the middle of a huge and unroaded forest tract was a bit unnerving. As I grew more confident of my map reading and compass skills, plus keeping track of where I was in relation to my green Forest Service truck, I became more comfortable.

I talked Kaye into spending a week with me at Soap Creek. Although it was fairly primitive living, I thought she might enjoy the scenery and the logging camp lifestyle. There was no TV, and radio reception was problematical. There was no indoor plumbing, and the primitive outhouse was about fifty feet from the front door.

The evening entertainment was either reading or 'wildlife viewing'. The logging camp maintained an open pit trash and garbage dump a few miles down the road. Occasionally after dinner we would drive out to the pit to watch foraging black bears. There could be as many as five or six at one time, including a few cubs. It was entertaining to watch them forage for food scraps, play and sometimes fight over a particularly desirable delicacy.

One morning we noticed fresh bear tracks around the outhouse, and Kaye decided it was no longer prudent to visit the outhouse after dark! That was the only week she spent with me at the Soap Creek logging camp. Kaye was pregnant, so she was a bit uncomfortable anyway, and I understood.

The forest had experienced several lightning-caused fires in late August. I had not been called out to assist in fire suppression then, but I was eager to do so. Late one afternoon a severe lightning storm crossed the area. That evening I received a message via my portable Forest Service radio that we had a fire on the rim of the Stanislaus River canyon, close to the area in which I had been preparing the timber sale. My immediate boss, Harry Schimke, was sending a ten-man crew, convicts from the California penal system, to assist me in extinguishing the fire, plus a driver/liaison person.

I was given a general location of the fire and plotted it on my map. By the time the inmate crew arrived, it was dark. Those guys were a bit scary-looking, but they were probably as apprehensive as I was. These were urban-oriented guys, out of their element in the middle of a forest on a very dark night. I led with my pickup, and they followed me in their stake side truck out on a dirt road that I calculated would lead us to a jump-off point near the fire. We would walk in from there.

Harry had also sent shovels, axes, and McClouds (a fire line scraping tool), canteens of water, and two sack lunches for each inmate. I distributed the tools and lunches, and we headed into the forest toward the reported location of the fire.

It was about a four-mile hike through dense forest to the rim of the canyon. We had to skirt stands of brush or thick stands of young trees. As we worked our way around one such stand we spooked something very large, and very determined to exit the stand as quickly as it could. We couldn't see it, but we could sure hear it. There was a loud 'woof' and a great thrashing and crashing as the creature ploughed its way out of the thicket and away from us. I stopped, and the inmates froze in their tracks just behind me.

"What the hell was that, man?" one of them exclaimed.

"A black bear," I replied.

"Oh shit! Let's get out of here," another said.

They all grouped around me, and the rest of the way to the fire they followed very close behind and in silence – probably imagining monster bears.

As we got closer, I could see the glow of the fire against the night sky from vantage points along the way, so we worked our way towards it. We were all happy to find it – it had taken two hours.

The fire was a couple of acres in size. I indicated where I wanted the fire line, and the inmates worked hard all night with no sleep. They cut, scraped and dug a good fire line around it, and by morning we had reinforced the line and worked inside it to mop up any hot spots. Soon after our lunch and in the early afternoon all the hot spots appeared to finally be out; I could not find any more. Having a 're-kindle' on a wildfire you were sent to extinguish was a definite 'no-no'. After making sure everything was dead out, I decided it was safe to leave.

Now to find the trucks! I had taken some compass bearings going in the night before, so I ran the same bearing back, hoping I would intersect the road near the trucks. As we hiked, nothing looked familiar and the inmates were getting anxious. Everything looked different in the daylight.

After nearly two hours of hiking, they were again following really close behind me. No risk of anyone running; no one wanted to be lost in this wilderness. I could hear them mumbling to each other behind me.

"I hope the man knows where he's going," one said.

"I think the ranger's lost, man," another added.

"This ain't the right way," was another opinion.

I could feel the tension growing and the murmurs were getting more frequent and louder. About the time they were close to panic, we emerged from the dense forest and onto the road. *Whew!*

There is not a more welcoming sight to a hiker, hunter or forester than to step out of a deep wood onto a road they thought should be, and hoped and prayed would be, there. Looking to my right, I was grateful to see the trucks about two hundred feet away! I smiled and acted like this was normal and routine. The inmates were greatly relieved, and so was I.

I radioed in to the ranger district and told them we had made it out OK. Harry congratulated me on a good job. Harry was the district timber management assistant (TMA) and my supervisor. He was not a professional forester but rather a 'technician' who had worked his was up though the ranks. He was one of the brightest and most competent bosses I worked with during my career. I learned a lot from Harry Schimke.

Often I found that long-term Forest Service employees who had hired on as teenagers stuck with it and moved up on the basis of their native abilities, usually on the same national forest; these people were very competent and knowledgeable. I soon formed the opinion that they constituted the bedrock of the forest, and newer employees looked to them for leadership, especially during fires and other times of crisis. They trained and educated new district rangers and other college-trained professionals. I determined I would listen to and learn from Harry and others like him as my career developed.

The district ranger of the Calaveras District was Billy Lunsford. He was a quiet, effective manager, and he made it a pleasure to be a part of his district team. Billy arrived on the district about the same time as I. His career goal was to be a district ranger, and now that he had achieved it, he told me he would likely be around for a long time. He remained there as district ranger for the rest of his career and retired twenty-plus years later.

It was highly unusual in the Forest Service for a person to remain in any professional position that long, and the practice was discouraged. Billy Lunsford was a man who knew exactly what he wanted. He died in November 2004 at the age of seventy-eight. I was saddened by his death. I had always intended to return to the area to see him. I admired and liked the man.

Our first child, Shannon Kaye, was born June 3, 1961, in San Andreas. She was healthy and alert from the moment of birth. Suddenly I was a dad!

We had rented a small apartment, an old, converted doctor's office, with a parking lot for a front yard. Kaye had experienced morning sickness throughout the pregnancy and was often cooped up in the apartment alone when I was in the field. Her labor and the delivery had been long and difficult. Kaye's mother arranged for a flight from Southern California in a single engine, private airplane to help her for a couple of weeks after Shannon arrived. She was of great assistance and a comfort to Kaye.

Shannon was a happy, easy-to-care-for baby, and we thought all babies were that way.

Mad River Ranger District, Six Rivers National Forest, CA 1961-1962

In late August of 1961, I was promoted to a GS-9, Timber Management Assistant (TMA) on the remote Mad River Ranger District in Northern California. My salary was $6,900 per annum. We were coming up in the world salary wise! Forest Service folks in central California viewed the Six Rivers Forest to be on the edge of the world and not a desirable assignment.

Shannon was three months old. Our small apartment in San Andreas contained only the minimum furniture; at that point in our lives we had few possessions. We were able to get them all in a U-Haul trailer, which we hooked up to our Nash Rambler, and we left for the north end of the state. When we arrived at the highway intersection to turn onto the road to Mad River, it was late afternoon, and hot.

The car did not have air-conditioning, and the drive up the narrow road to Mad River took another two hours. We finally arrived in the early evening. As good as Shannon had been about traveling, she was now uncomfortable, tired and crying. The first people to greet us at the ranger station were Leo and Areta Porterfield. Leo immediately reached in and took Shannon out of the car, walked her around, and cooed to her until she quieted. Areta invited us over for a spaghetti dinner that evening at their tiny government-provided residence on the 'compound'. Living on a ranger station compound was like that, folks looked after one another.

We became good friends with the Porterfields, and our careers were destined to cross paths again on the Inyo National Forest a few years later.

The community of Mad River clustered around a combined gas

75

station, tavern and tiny country store. That was it. Most of the citizens worked in the logging or sawmill industry. Loggers wearing trousers 'stagged off' at mid calf, held up by red suspenders were customers of the tavern, whose floor was pock marked by the steel spiked or 'corked' boots of those that worked in the woods. They were often transported to work in the 'crummy', usually a beat up and dirty four-wheel suburban or van. Terms vaguely familiar to me were the norm here. Colorful, descriptive logging jargon such as school-marm, whistlepunk, longbutt, swamper, tin pants, widow-maker, and choker setter was the language of Mad River. I was impressed by these hard working, hard living people who engaged in their dangerous occupations in the woods or sawmills every day.

The Mad River Ranger Station and compound consisted of a large warehouse and several residences. It was situated on a ridge or divide between the Mad and the Van Duzen River canyons. The TMA residence was plain but of newer vintage and sat on the very top of the ridge with views into the valley of each river canyon – a very scenic and attractive setting.

The downside of the ranger station location, and it was a significant downside, was the two-hour drive, one way, west to Fortuna or Eureka for groceries and all other major shopping. It was a narrow, winding mountain road with sections of oiled gravel and sections of untreated, dusty gravel. Meeting logging trucks on sharp corners was a common occurrence. We shopped once a month, and it was an all-day endeavor. It took some adjustments to live at the Mad River Ranger Station.

However, in the evening we could see many deer that would come out to browse in the 'glades' (open spaces of grasslands in the dense oak stands that predominated the south facing slopes), and there were quail everywhere. Not a bad place for a forester and hunter!

My job was to head up the district's timber management

program. This entailed preparation of future timber sales by locating and laying them out, cruising for a volume estimate and appraising them to establish a minimum bid. I was also responsible for administering the contracts for the harvest of the existing active sales. I worked directly for Hatch Graham, the district ranger, and had two employees to help me.

I enjoyed preparing future sales the most. This was Douglas-fir country, much different to the more open pine country of the Stanislaus. On north-facing slopes the Doug-fir, as we called it, grew in heavy, dense stands with trees of thirty inches or greater in diameter. Douglas-fir seedlings did not tolerate much shade, so small clear-cuts were the favored silvicultural prescription to ensure successful reforestation.

We had a five-year plan for future sales and harvest. Many of the areas were located beyond the end of existing roads. Therefore, sale reconnaissance and preparation involved hiking into the proposed sale area, taking maps and aerial photographs as an aid in evaluating the appropriateness for timber harvest, then delineating harvest blocks or marking individual trees for harvest. I would locate and designate an access road using an Abney level (a survey instrument) and compass, and flag its location with brightly colored plastic surveyors' ribbon for future construction.

Just before leaving San Andreas we had acquired a dog. He was a cross between a German shorthaired pointer and a Weimaraner. He had the distinctive Weimaraner 'gray ghost' color, so we named him Smokey. He was just a pup of five months, but I took him with me on my sale reconnaissance excursions. I recall him initially struggling to cross the bottoms of the V-shaped draws of that steep Six Rivers country. After a month or so he was ranging the hillsides at a fast lope, a gray flash ahead in the trees and brush. He was good company on those long days alone in the middle of nowhere. I did have to break him from chasing deer though.

An Encounter with the Timber Imperative

During my career I thought of myself as one of the 'good guys'. I tried hard to do the right thing in caring for the land and natural resources of the forests that belonged to all citizens. This, I knew, was the heritage of the Forest Service. The agency was born in 1905 to counter the accelerating exploitation of these public domain lands by interests with a short-term time horizon and quick profits in mind.

My notion of who I was and what I was about was challenged at times by the publics with whom I worked. The timber industry often accused me of being too conservative regarding cutting trees; environmentalists usually held that I wanted to cut too many trees at the expense of fish, wildlife, watershed and roadless values.

At this early point in my career, I thought my charge was basic and clear: My first priority in administering timber sales was to protect the basic resources of the soil, water, wildlife habitat and the trees to be left to perpetuate the next forest, and in a larger context the ecosystem.

I had inherited the administration of the huge Upper Van Duzen Timber Sale. It was a fifty-million board-foot, multi-year sale. It had been sold several years previous in a manner that the investors who constructed the sawmill were assured of a supply of timber for many years. For comparison, the volume we normally offered for bid on the district was five to fifteen million.

This was a huge sale, with an implied guarantee of the volume to be harvested. The problem was that the volume estimates for the Upper Van Duzen had been overly optimistic. The sale was seriously undercutting its advertised volume, thus the Forest Service was obligated to make more area and trees available to make up the shortfall. To make matters worse, the sale purchaser – the owner of the newer sawmill on the lower section of the Van Duzen River – was more than a year behind on the erosion control measures (placing water diversions in tractor skid trails), and slash

78

cleanup (piling and burning brush) as specified in the timber sale contract. It was a mess, far short of compliance with the contract. I was appalled when I first saw the situation. I did not tolerate this on my previous assignments on the Stanislaus Forest, and I was not going to tolerate it here.

I had repeatedly asked the purchaser, both verbally and formally by letter, to catch up with the back erosion control work before the winter rains set in, and to get the slash piled for winter burning. I received promises and a few halfhearted, token efforts. It was clear he was hoping to get by. *I am being tested*, I thought. So I drafted a letter for the district ranger's signature and sent it to the purchaser. Under his authority the ranger shut down logging operations for repeated noncompliance with the contract and set a date for this backlog of work to be completed before logging could resume.

One morning shortly thereafter I was catching up with some paperwork in the office when my phone rang. Our receptionist said it was the owner-operator of the Van Duzen Sawmill – the sale purchaser. He had wanted to speak with the district ranger, who was out of the office for the day, but settled for me. *Oops, something is up. This is not good*, I thought.

I detected a smirk in his voice as he informed me, "Well, Ron, it seems the Assistant Regional Forester (ARF) in charge of timber management from the regional office in San Francisco has just flown in to our airstrip at the mill. He wants you to come down and talk to him about the Van Duzen Timber Sale."

I was stunned. I knew I was in trouble. A grade GS-9 forester in the middle of nowhere getting an unscheduled visit from a 'GS-gee whiz' top echelon of management in San Francisco was like an unannounced visit from God.

"OK, in about a half-hour or so," I stammered.

The whole situation was so unusual I called the forest supervisor's office in Eureka and informed the forest timber management officer of the request. He was not pleased.

"This is highly irregular and the forest supervisor will not like it," he said. "But go ahead, I'll see if I can get loose here and come out and join you."

Eureka was a hard two hours' drive away. I knew he would arrive too late to support me – I was on my own.

I went to the mill and both men were sitting in the owner's cluttered, dusty sawmill office waiting for me. The ARF introduced himself then bluntly asked, "Why have you and your ranger shut down the Upper Van Duzen sale, Mr. McCormick?"

I reiterated the long history of this purchaser ignoring and failing to fulfill contract requirements and pointed out that fall and winter rains were not far in the future.

The ARF began his lecture, "Ron, this mill is almost totally dependent on a supply of national forest timber, and when the mill is down, most of the community ends up out of work." He then added the admonition, "This mill must have a dependable supply of logs."

I responded, respectfully I thought. "Yes, sir, I understand and do not take the shut-down of the sale lightly." I quickly added, "After repeated attempts, this was a last resort measure to get the sale purchaser's attention and encourage him to follow contract requirements."

The ARF frowned at me, and the mill owner grinned, obviously enjoying my discomfort.

The ARF's eyes bored into me, and he said with emphasis, "This mill and community are of primary importance!"

I bristled and said, "I believe my primary responsibility is to see that the resources of the national forest and the Upper Van Duzen River are protected." I emphatically added, "The purchaser can get the logs coming to the mill if he would make a good faith effort to catch up erosion control and brush disposal requirements."

The ARF looked at me and frowned again. This was obviously

not the reply he wanted. The mill owner continued to grin.

I made a request of my own. "Sir, the sale area is less than an hour up the river. I have my pickup, let's take a ride up there and you can see for yourself." I added, "There is just a blatant lack of adherence to the erosion control and slash disposal work clearly specified in the contract this man signed." I gestured toward the mill owner.

The ARF looked at me a bit surprised and explained, rather lamely I thought, "I have to get back to the regional office for an important meeting, but I will fly over the sale on the way back."

Yeah, right! I thought. *A lot you are going to see from six thousand feet!* But I didn't say it. I was soon excused. *Wow!* I thought as I drove back to the Ranger Station, *is this what it takes to ascend to the highest ranks of the Forest Service?*

Two months later I received an unsolicited, directed reassignment without promotion to the Big Bear Ranger District on the San Bernardino National Forest in Southern California.

The 'take away' lesson for me was that when push came to shove, the big business of timber sales in the Forest Service often overrode other considerations, in spite of our mantra of 'multiple use'. I began to think of this as the 'timber imperative'. This hard reality was to be reinforced in the years ahead and assignments yet to come.

I often wondered how a mill owner in Northern California had the influence to get a personal visit from the regional director of timber management. Later I was told that the ARF and the mill owner had attended Oregon State University together. I never could confirm that, but it would explain how the mill owner could arrange such a visit. The ARF went on to have a distinguished career, culminating in Washington, D.C. as director of timber management for all the national forests in the nation.

In 1998 Carol and I took a nostalgic trip, visiting several national forests and stations in California where I had previously been assigned. We towed our travel trailer and stayed a few nights in a small campground on the Van Duzen River near the Mad River Ranger Station. The highway was better, but little else had changed. At the site of the sawmill all that remained was a rusting 'teepee' sawdust burner. I decided not to visit the area of the old Upper Duzen Timber Sale.

Big Bear Ranger District - San Bernardino National Forest, CA 1962-1968

I had been abruptly reassigned. We left Mad River in late October 1962 in a steady rain. This time we elected to hire a moving van as we had accumulated more furniture and other 'stuff'. The storm turned out to be a major one with driving rain and heavy winds. We learned later that the Northern California streams and rivers flooded and much damage occurred to structures and roads. I thought of the Van Duzen Timber Sale and the skid trails without water bars.

We drove out of the storm just south of Sacramento. The sun was shining, the sky a brilliant blue, and life was looking better.

Climbing the City Creek grade out of San Bernardino and heading up the mountains toward Big Bear Lake, I looked at the steep, chaparral choked hillsides and thought, *Oh No! What have I gotten us into?* Then we topped out at the 6,800-foot elevation level at Big Bear Lake Dam; a large, placid lake surrounded by pine-covered mountains greeted us. Kaye and I concluded that this might just be all right after all!

My new position was assistant district ranger (ADR), and in those days the ADR had line authority. Although this was a directed reassignment with no promotion, I took solace in the notion that it at least seemed like a step up. The district was well balanced in natural resources. It had stands of ponderosa pine, Jeffrey pine, and white fir surrounding the lake, an abundance of wildlife, commercial grazing activity, and outstanding outdoor recreation opportunities.

The major activity at Big Bear was management of a large outdoor recreation program, including campgrounds, three ski areas, and over four hundred summer homes. Administration of 'special use permits' for other private uses of national forest lands was also an important job at Big Bear. These were in my area of responsibility and all new to me, and promised to open another world.

The district operated many campgrounds around and near the lake; the area was heavily visited and used by residents of the Los Angeles basin. The locals called these weekend visitors 'flat-landers'. The east side of the district made a transition to a pinion pine, sagebrush high desert ecosystem as it dropped down the mountains to the Mojave Desert. The 150,000-acre district offered a very diversified, attractive and interesting piece of country.

Kaye was happy because we were in Southern California and within a few hours' drive of her parents and her sister's family in the L.A. area. The Big Bear area contained three small communities around the lake, Fawnskin, Big Bear City, and Big Bear Lake, which together offered good schools and shopping. The lake offered good trout fishing in summer and duck hunting in the fall – a very nice place to live and raise a family. We were all happy, and I felt as content as I had ever been with our situation and my job.

Sometime later, Don Bauer, forest supervisor of the San Bernardino National Forest, told me he had received a letter from Wes Spinney, supervisor of the Six Rivers National Forest, about me and my reassignment. Although I had left under a cloud, Mr. Spinney was very complimentary regarding the work I had done on the Mad River Ranger District. I began to feel a bit better about the entire event.

We rented a small, modest, two-bedroom home. After a year the owner sold it, and as we didn't yet have enough money for a down payment for a home of our own, we rented another two-bedroom house; it wasn't quite as nice as the first one.

One day Kaye came into the office very excited. "I won a house!" she exclaimed.

"What?" I said in disbelief. "What happened? How can this be?" We hadn't entered a contest to my knowledge.

Kaye explained that in paying the propane bill she entered a drawing or raffle for a vacation cabin the propane company was giving away as part of a promotion. Now I was also excited!

Kaye was always quite lucky, and this was a stroke of especially good fortune. As we learned the details, it was not quite as good as it first sounded. It turned out that the propane company had awarded three two-bedroom cabins to lucky participants nationwide, but they were really prefabricated cabins manufactured by a company located in the Southeast. We were told we had to arrange for and pay to have the truckload of building materials shipped to the site. We didn't have a lot to build it on, nor, for that matter, the money to have the material shipped.

I talked to the local propane company manager, telling him of our situation. He finally agreed to pick up the freight charges. The cabin materials were shipped to San Bernardino by rail, and then trucked to Big Bear. We had a huge truckload of building materials, from siding to rafters, delivered to and dumped in the back yard of our rental house. What to do now?

We put some money down on a small lot at the east end of the lake in a neighborhood of cheaper homes. I hired a person to help dig footings and pour a foundation. Over the course of a summer I worked evenings and weekends hauling the material to the lot. Kaye also helped when she could, and the little house began to take shape.

We had lots of help from friends. Mom and Dad had retired and left Chagrin Falls to live in Yucaipa, located at the base of the San Bernardino Mountains. On weekends Dad came up and helped me erect the prefabricated roof trusses. We constructed the little home and finished and painted the outside. We didn't have the funds to finish the inside, so we sold it "as is". We netted enough to pay off the debts, and saved a small nest egg for a down payment on a future home for our family.

District Ranger!

A district ranger was and remains the most coveted position in the Forest Service. Many aspire, but few are chosen.

Every professional Forest Service employee hoped to be selected, and so did I. The position is steeped in the mystique, romance and lore of the U.S. Forest Service. For years I had held an image in my head of a solitary figure on a mountaintop, reins of a trusty horse in one hand, the other holding binoculars to view his domain.

After a couple of years the Big Bear district ranger, for whom I worked, was promoted and transferred to a larger ranger district on the Sierra National Forest to the north. He recommended to Forest Supervisor Bauer that I succeed him in the position. At the time I was not aware I was even being considered. In those days the regional office (San Francisco, in the case of California) masterminded all career placements in the state.

Apparently I had made a good impression on Supervisor Bauer, and he had recommended me to the regional office. I was offered the position with a promotion to GS-11. I was a district ranger! I had reached that legendary and coveted position and achieved a major career goal.

It can't get much better than this, I thought. And I was right.

It was very unusual then, and even to this day, to be promoted to a district ranger position from within the same ranger district. I was very fortunate, and very grateful. This was finally a promotion, and the move was only a couple of miles to the government house provided for the district ranger on the district compound. This plain, but newer three-bedroom house was located on top of a ridge overlooking the ranger station and compound with an outstanding view of Big Bear Lake. The dark cloud of Mad River had totally dissipated.

I felt good about being selected, and about being ready for this responsibility. I knew I had good support from the staff people I worked with on the district, who now would be working for me. I knew the district and its resources, and key contacts in the communities, including the mayors, chamber of commerce leaders and the editor of the local newspaper. The transition was relatively easy.

Forest Supervisor Don Bauer took me under his wing.

"Ranger McCormick, do you have a 'key man' list?" he asked during one of his visits.

"A what list?" I responded. I had never heard the term.

"A list of the influential people in the communities around Bear Valley. The people that make things happen."

"No, I don't," I admitted.

"Well, develop one, and run it by me," he directed. "Always remember that understanding and acceptance are critical before you can expect support of Forest Service programs from the community. Make sure you visit key people and organizations informally and on a regular basis," he concluded.

"Yes, sir," I said. "That makes good sense to me."

And it did. Don Bauer was way ahead of much of the organization on public involvement. We later organized 'show me' field trips to review our project plans with local interest groups, including Sierra Club representatives from cities in the valley below. His guidance and training helped form my notion of the effectiveness of full public participation in national forest resource protection and management.

Fitch's Eagle

Steve Fitch was a college student and worked his summers as a seasonal employee on the district. I was impressed with his energy and enthusiasm, and upon his graduation from Oregon State University as a forester, we hired him as a permanent employee and junior forester.

One evening near dusk my family was seated at the dinner table when I heard a vehicle drive up the hill and into the driveway. *What now?* I thought. Disturbances in the evening were not uncommon. There was a loud and urgent knock at the door.

"Ron, Ron, it's an eagle!" someone exclaimed. It sounded like Fitch. I opened the door and Steve stood there, obviously excited.

"What in the world is going on?" I asked.

"I was driving to the station and I think I hit a golden eagle," Steve explained hurriedly. "It flew right into the front of the car and bounced off into the sagebrush. I don't think its dead. Can you help me find and catch it? Maybe we can save it."

"OK," I agreed. "But wait just a second."

I asked Kaye for an old blanket, thinking that if the eagle just had a broken wing, we could capture it without further harm and take it to the local veterinarian. She found one, and we hurried off to the place of the incident, about a mile away.

Night was approaching, and we were rapidly losing light. We spread out and searched through the dense sagebrush. Steve hollered, "Here it is, here it is!"

I ran to him in time to see a large, brown, feathery shape scurry off. *It could be an eagle*, I thought. We chased it through the brush, finally cornering the creature against a log. It was now nearly dark, but we managed to throw the blanket over the shape and wrap up the large, struggling bird. We couldn't get a good look at it.

"Let's take it up to the house. I can turn on the outside floodlight, and we'll take a look," I suggested.

At the house we set the blanket on the driveway under the

bright light. The creature was fighting and squawking under the blanket, and an unfamiliar and distinctly unpleasant odor filled the air. *What in the world?* I thought. I anticipated the magnificent form of a golden or bald eagle to emerge, but as we pulled the blanket off, out tumbled the ugliest, nastiest, most angry turkey vulture I had ever seen. It seemed to be covered with excrement, and it just reeked. A look of amazement and incredulity crossed Steve's face. I began to laugh, and finally Steve joined in. To this day when we recount the story, it brings tears of laughter to our eyes.

Steve went on to have a very successful career, including two assignments as district ranger, a Washington office assignment, forest supervisor of the National Forests of Florida, and finally forest supervisor of the large Shasta-Trinity National Forest in Northern California. I see him from time to time and he is still full of energy and enthusiasm.

Mike's Arrival

Michael J. McCormick was born March 27, 1963, while we were living at Big Bear. There was not yet a hospital in the community, so he was delivered in the hospital at Apple Valley down on the desert side of the mountains. Shannon now had a baby brother, and I had a son.

The western movie star and singer Roy Rogers owned an old, rundown resort on Big Bear Lake. It was located on national forest land and authorized under a special use permit. It consisted of a boat dock, boat rentals and a bait shop. I had met Mr. Rogers over lunch one day to discuss the Forest Service's desire to both upgrade and modernize the resort or dismantle it to make room for a public lakeside picnic area. I found Roy Rogers easy to talk to and a true gentleman – it was a pleasure to work with him. It was clear he had no real interest in the old resort and eventually decided to remove it. In the meantime, his interest and energy was devoted to developing the 'Roy Rogers Museum' in Apple Valley.

One Saturday, when Mike was about two years old, Kaye and I decided to take the kids to see the newly completed museum. I was carrying Mike as we entered, and for some reason the swinging glass entry door hit Mike on the back of his head as it closed behind us. Mike hollered, more surprised and frightened than hurt, and began to cry. I was walking Mike around, trying to get him calmed down, when Roy Rogers emerged from a nearby office. He recognized me and held out his arms for Mike. He took Mike and walked him around the museum until he settled down. I am sure Mike doesn't remember the event, but I sure do.

Fire on the Mountain

The Forest Service in general and in Southern California in particular, all employees were trained in fighting forest fires and were expected to be available to respond when called. This was in the early 1960s before formal fire 'overhead' teams were organized.

I had received considerable training and had, from time to time, been assigned to several large fires throughout the state. The Forest Service in Southern California placed considerable emphasis on fire training, evaluation, and rating of positions for which you had become qualified. By 1964 I had achieved the 'Red Card' rating of sector boss. This position in a fire fighting organization was responsible for a specific portion or sector of a fire line to construct and defend. From one to several twenty-man crews were assigned, plus equipment, to a sector. In late September of 1964, I was assigned to the Coyote Fire on the Los Padre National Forest, located in the mountains just behind the costal community of Santa Barbara.

I arrived at the fire camp, which was in a polo field on the edge of the community just below the mountains, and the fire. It was smoky in the camp as a 'Santa Ana', or east wind, was pushing the fire down the mountain and toward the town. In fact, at one point the fire made a run to the outskirts of the fire camp and covered it with smoke and ash. Nearly five hundred firefighters were temporarily evacuated.

I was assigned to be on the nightshift as sector boss with two crews of twenty men each. Our assignment was to improve and hold a previously constructed firebreak, called a 'pre-attack line', on the ridge just north of a depression or dip in the ridge called Romero Saddle. We had a moderate east wind which was pushing the fire down the mountainside away from us and toward Santa Barbara. We worked all night cleaning up, widening, and generally reinforcing the line. I had been informed that at some time in the late night or early morning the east wind would ease, and the more normal west wind from the ocean would begin to dominate. Following our night's work, my instructions were to be at Romero Saddle about nine a.m. to meet a replacement crew being transported up the mountain for the shift change.

I had the crew in the saddle at the appointed time, but the replacement crew was late, as was more typical than not in the early stages of a large campaign fire. Jerry Berry, the line boss, and a well-known and respected Southern California firefighter, came by and said the shift change was going a bit slow and to continue to work on the line until they showed up.

It was past midmorning when the trucks with relief crews aboard finally arrived. My crew was tired, dirty and hungry. We had been on the line for about fifteen hours. Long shifts were also typical in the early stages of a large fire. In the meantime, the east winds had abated, and it was eerily calm. Fire behavior below us was becoming more erratic, and I could see flare-ups and small uphill runs in the large patches of unburned fuel below us. *I don't like the looks of this*, I thought.

We boarded the trucks and made the return trip to the fire camp. It was almost noon, and I could feel and smell an ocean breeze; the wind had shifted.

There was suddenly a commotion in the fire camp, and people and equipment were moving with urgency. I went over to the 'plans' tent to see what was going on.

A strong west wind had pushed the fire back up the hill into and though Romero Saddle, the place we had left an hour or so before. I knew there were several fresh crews there on the fire line getting organized to go to work.

In researching exactly what happened after my crew boarded the trucks and left Romero Saddle, I discovered the following vivid and chilling description in the online magazine *Santa Barbara Outdoors*, and I quote from that article:

Line Boss Jerry Berry put out a call on the radio network. There is an urgency in his voice. 'An unknown number of men have been trapped by a flare-up on the north side – as many as 30 men may be involved.'

Near Romero Saddle the second crew works feverishly to keep a fire burning in Romero Canyon from crossing the Camino Cielo (road) and burning into the Santa Ynez drainage.

The crew is split up. One group heads to a high point above Toro Saddle, and commences backfiring operations there. The remainder, from Klamath National Forest, stay at Romero Saddle to continue firing out this area. The Klamath crew has only just arrived at the fire at 12:30....

At Romero Saddle the flames pour in from three sides, trapping four of the firemen from Yreka as they hack out a fire line nearby. Before they can run, it is on them, the flames drifting across the dirt road which is their only hope of escape.

Three of the men fling themselves in the dirt below the road. But the fourth, John Patterson, hesitates, then yells at the others, 'Come on! We can make it this way,' he shouts as he starts up the road.

'Stop!' yells one of the others, Dave Alberts. But Patterson runs on.

For a half hour the other three men grovel in the dirt, covering themselves up with it the best they can. Patterson is 400 feet away, dead.

The other three were badly burned, but survived.

The following evening on the way to our shift assignment, we stopped briefly at the site of the incident in Romero Saddle. An investigation team was on site and stakes were in the ground at various locations identifying the location of the victims. I can vividly remember seeing pieces of burned Levi's near one of the stakes.

The Coyote Fire was to become infamous in the history of fires of the west. It eventually burned 67,000 acres and was controlled about a month later. At least twenty homes were destroyed, including the mansion of Avery Brundage, the president of the International Olympic Committee. At one time there were over a thousand people on the fire. There were thirty injuries, and one death, forty-five-year-old John Patterson, a firefighter from the Northern California town of Yreka.

Forest Supervisor Don Bauer

In order to have a successful career in the Forest Service, it is helpful, almost essential, to have a mentor and advocate. Don Bauer was mine. Don had been both a district ranger and fire management officer on the San Bernardino Forest before being appointed forest supervisor. He was a philosopher, educator, and coach. His ever-present pipe completed the image.

Don could talk, lecture, and pontificate at length. Some of my contemporaries grew weary of it, but I never did. After a day in the field, we would sit in front of the ranger station in my pickup and talk on into the evening. He did most of the talking. Subjects were mostly Forest Service: multiple use, public involvement and support, goals and objectives, supervision skills, and what wine to serve at an important dinner. (He favored Cabernet Sauvignon, and instructed me on its correct pronunciation.) I liked the man and enjoyed listening to this fount of wisdom and knowledge. I soaked it up and learned a great deal from him. He was the greatest single influence on my career.

When I think of Big Bear, I recall it as a rich, fulfilling and rewarding experience and a special time of our lives. I believe, and hope, that Kaye, Shannon, and Mike share that feeling.

In the fall of 1968, I received a call from Supervisor Bauer. He informed me that I was being offered the Recreation Staff Officer position on the Inyo National Forest, headquartered in Bishop, California on the east side of the Sierra Nevada. The family had twenty-four hours to decide. For the first time we had a choice. We answered yes. During my acceptance call to Don Bauer, he asked rhetorically, "So you really want to hitch your career wagon to the recreation star?" I really had not thought of it that way, but I replied in the affirmative.

Inyo National Forest, CA 1968-1974

During my career I was very fortunate to be assigned to some of the most dramatically scenic locations in the western United States. Bishop, California and the Inyo National Forest may just top the list.

The naturalist John Muir called the region "an area of wonderful contrasts, hot deserts bordered by snow-laden mountains, cinders and ashes scattered on glacier-polished pavement, frost and fire working together in the making of beauty." The local Paiute Indian Tribe called the place 'Inyo'. In their language 'Inyo' meant 'dwelling place of the great spirit'.

The national forest spanned a 165-mile-long stretch of the crest of the eastern escarpment of the Sierra Nevada Mountains, running from Lone Pine north to the California-Nevada border. It encompassed two million acres of snow-capped peaks, laced with four hundred lakes and a thousand miles of streams. The region contained the John Muir, Minaret and Golden Trout Wildernesses. It was a dramatic and majestic place.

Kaye, Shannon, Mike and I moved to Bishop in the late fall of 1968. It was a nice town of about four thousand people located in the heart of the Owens Valley between the Sierra Nevada and White Mountain ranges. Thanks to Kaye's good fortune, and our mutual hard work, we now had funds for a down payment. We purchased our first home in a new development on Underwood Lane for about $27,000. That seemed like an enormous amount of money then, and we were apprehensive, but we plunged ahead. (A trip though Bishop in September 2004 had similar homes in the neighborhood listed for sale at over $400,000.) This was a lateral transfer, and my salary was $11,843 per annum.

Daniel C. McCormick Arrives

Dan was born the following spring on April 6, 1969 in the local Bishop hospital. He was delivered by Dr. Denton, who became our family doctor. Dr. Denton was also the official doctor on some Forest Service pack trips via horseback and mule far back into the wilderness – a good safety measure. Due to our nomadic lifestyle with the Forest Service, each of our children was born in a different community, but all in California.

Dan was a good baby and grew up to be a pleasant child. He visited other families in the neighborhood on his own, and they all told me they enjoyed Dan's impromptu visits. The three kids' pet mallard duck, Daffy, followed Dan everywhere.

The Inyo was and is all about public outdoor recreation. A five-hour drive from the Los Angeles basin, it is one of Southern California's outdoor playgrounds. The Inyo is one of the most heavily visited national forests in the United States, hosting five million visitors annually. Its recreation facilities include over a hundred campgrounds and two large ski resorts – Mammoth

Mountain and June Mountain. The forest contains over one million acres of designated wilderness accessed by thirty-six trailheads, and over fifty resorts and lodges on public land operated under special use permits from the Forest Service. It is quite an outdoor recreation plant and operation.

My assignment was the forest recreation staff officer to the forest supervisor, responsible for the smooth and efficient operation of this large and diverse public outdoor recreation facility. It was a great job, one of the best in my thirty-three-year career. In part this positive memory was due to the magnificent setting of this forest, part to the friendly people of Bishop, but largely attributable to the people with whom I worked, several of whom became lifelong friends: Everett Towle, the forest supervisor; Bruce Pewitt, the forest engineer; and Jack Dinwiddie, the forest administrative officer.

When I composed this chapter on September 13, 2004, Carol and I were camped at OH! Ridge campground on June Lake in the Inyo National Forest. The next morning as the sun rose, we watched the morning sunlight creep down the side of the Sierra peaks to the west, soon to touch the placid waters of June Lake. It was an enchanting fall morning in the eastern Sierra. The air was crisp and clean, and the aspens streaked with gold. I was reminded of what I liked so much about this country.

Everyone in the family liked Bishop and the Owens Valley. After living there for six years, the place really became home. Kaye sang with the local chapter of Sweet Adelines, Mike played little league baseball, and I coached then later managed his team, with the help of Jack Dinwiddie. Shannon seemed to like school there and did very well. Dan was a young child and had the run of the neighborhood.

Joe Radel was the forest supervisor when I first arrived. He was a good and honest man who loved the Inyo and had a vision of enhancing forest visitors' outdoor recreation experience with more and better interpretation of the geologic events that created the striking landscape. It was largely through his efforts that funds were secured for the modern visitor information center that was constructed in Mammoth Lakes. He also fostered the creation of the Eastern Sierra Interpretive Association, a private, nonprofit organization that could sell brochures, books and other materials about the forest to the public at a reasonable price.

Later, Jack Dinwiddie transferred in as the forest administrative officer. Smart, a bit calculating yet a creative thinker, Jack reveled in solving problems and developing creative solutions. His interests were much broader than just personnel and budgets, the usual realm of an administrative officer. He didn't see any need to limit himself to helping solve problems in just those areas and was not bashful in offering his ideas and advice to me on recreation matters. His gift of unconventional, 'outside the box' thinking characterized both his career and life.

Bruce Pewitt soon arrived as the new forest engineer. He clearly was an engineer to the core. He came up through the Forest Service working on summer survey crews just out of high school. The Forest Service recognized the potential in Bruce and encouraged him to attend college and get a Degree in Civil Engineering, meanwhile promising summer employment until he graduated. Also very intelligent, he held strong opinions on a wide-ranging span of subjects, and he was eager to share them. Bruce was multi-talented. An excellent mechanic, he has restored several classic cars, and an excellent woodworker and cabinetmaker who has remodeled several houses. His talents as an engineer, mechanic and cabinetmaker are all characterized by high standards and a marked impatience with shoddy work.

Jack and Bruce both purchased homes in our neighborhood and moved in with their families. Thus we were co-workers, neighbors, and over time, close friends.

Everett Towle succeeded the retired Joe Radel as the forest

supervisor of the Inyo. A native of Maine, Ev's taciturn manner concealed a sharp mind and clever wit. His conservative appearance and demeanor disguised an ability to think both creatively and strategically, and a willingness to take risks. He was an excellent forest supervisor. Under Ev's leadership, we were to become the core of a very good forest management team of staff and rangers. Some later referred to the team and those times as 'Camelot'.

Perhaps the most significant achievement of our time there together was the development of a system of modern sewage disposal systems, along with campground reconstruction and upgrading at Bishop Creek, Mammoth Lakes, June Lake Loop, and other areas of concentrated recreation facilities and use.

The signing into law of the Water Pollution Control Act of 1972 provided us the opportunity. This legislation was commonly known as the 'Clean Water Act'. Its stated objectives were "the restoration and maintenance of chemical, physical and biological integrity of the nation's waters..."

Through a team effort we demonstrated to Washington, D.C. officials that the antiquated vault toilets of our campgrounds were leaking and contributing to the pollution of the pristine streams and lakes that were the key attributes of the Inyo National Forest.

It was controversial, but we had the facts and eventually garnered a large share of the total amount of pollution abatement funds available to all the national forests in the nation. Over the next two years we constructed sewage collection and treatment systems and reconstructed many campgrounds. In this large and intensive effort over a period of three years, we protected the water quality of eastern Sierra streams and lakes, and totally upgraded the forest's outdoor recreation facilities. Forest Engineer Bruce Pewitt and his staff led that amazing project.

Most of the forest's old campgrounds had been constructed in the Civilian Conservation Corp era in the 1930s, primarily for small automobiles and tent camping. Ted Rickford, the forest landscape architect, redesigned many of them, and we created new and larger facilities that could accommodate both tent campers and the larger recreation vehicles that were beginning to dominate the outdoor recreation scene.

A Baja Diversion

Jack and Bruce had an interest in the peninsula of Baja, California, Mexico. Frankly, I had never read or thought much about the place. Jack knew about the gray whale migration route from Alaskan waters down the west side of the peninsula, and Bruce had information that the dirt road (of Baja 1000 road race fame) traversing the length of the Baja was about to be upgraded and paved. They had the bright idea of acquiring motorcycles and riding down toward the tip of Baja to experience the old route before it was gone forever. This held the promise of a great adventure.

We asked Ev for three weeks off to make the trip. To have three staff officers on leave at the same time was going to be an impact and burden on him, and we knew it, but he graciously consented. In retrospect I think we overestimated our importance to the forest's operation.

It was an eventful trip, replete with spills, interesting cultural interaction, and stunning scenery. The highlight was camping for a few days on a beach fronting the Bay of Conception on the Sea of Cortez, south of the small town of Mulege about halfway down the peninsula. We had that portion of the bay to ourselves, our only company was a Mexican shrimp boat that fished at night and anchored in the bay during the day. This was truly an enchanted place – a turquoise sea in a desert setting.

The trip cemented our friendship, and thanks to Jack's efforts years later led each of us to own property in Baja. In recent years that Baja road was named Baja Route 1. It has now been realigned and paved. On a recent road trip down the Baja, Carol and I saw hundreds of RVs lining that same beach, side by side.

Special People of the Inyo

Each national forest, probably every enterprise of any size, has a select few who help ground the organization to reality and are the essence of the organization. They are usually not the bosses. One such person on the Inyo was Edwin C. Rockwell, known to all as 'Rocky'. A product of the Army's 10th Mountain Division during WWII, he came west and was the first snow ranger at Mammoth Mountain Ski Area, and in 1955 the first Forest Service employee to spend the winter in Mammoth Lakes. The town now hosts thousands during both summer and winter. Methodical and determined, Rocky always got the job done. He was instrumental in creating the Eastern Sierra Interpretive Association – initially running the operation out of his home. His special talent as a photographer was also recognized. In addition to his principle duties as assistant recreation staff, he became the forest photographer. His black and white and color photos now hang in Forest Service offices and employee homes – including my own. His dramatic photos include the Bristlecone Pine, Mt. Whitney, and Mt. Tom. Rocky was eighty-four at the time of this writing and still hiking the mountain trails of the Sierra and Inyo Mountains.

Another special person was Leo Porterfield. Our family met Leo and Areta upon our arrival at Mad River a few years and assignments earlier. We never forgot their kindness to us, and from the start we worked well together. Leo had once confided in me that his goal and dream job was to be the construction and maintenance foreman for the Inyo. The position entailed packing work crews, equipment and tenderfoots like me, and sometimes Bruce and Jack, into the wilderness, plus the care of the forest's seventy head of horses and mules.

When we arrived on the Inyo, Leo welcomed us with open arms, and I knew I had at least one supporter in my new assignment. Leo and his wife, Areta, had no children, but Leo loved kids. He always held and fussed over Shannon, Mike and

Dan. I am sure they remember him.

Leo was of stocky build with a double chin. His hands were scarred from years of outdoor work and tying packs on mules. He liked a drink of Old Crow bourbon before dinner and would lecture to those who would listen about the 'old Forest Service' and how the outfit was going to hell with the new generation. I would grin and bear it, but in retrospect he wasn't far off the mark. On the other hand, is it just that I am older now and like it better the way it was?

I made several pack trips into the wilderness areas with Leo and various ranger district representatives to inspect levels of use and bridge and trail conditions. Those were great trips, and a nice change from the office, where as a staff person I spent most of my time.

The clock never mattered to Leo. After packing and loading the mules, it would be ten a.m. before we were in the saddle and left the trailhead. Leo would ride through lunch hour, leading a string of four or five mules, and then ride through the dinner hour, determined to reach his destination for the night. About seven p.m. I'd ask, "Just how far is this campsite anyway?" (Are we there yet?)

Leo would just grunt something unintelligible. By now my knees, legs and butt were killing me, and I would have to step off the big palomino called Mexico and walk a ways to get the circulation back into my legs and rear. He usually headed for a campsite called 'Horse Heaven' or some place similar that had good pasture for the stock. We might make camp about eight p.m., strip the saddles off the horses and the packs off the mules, and then hobble the horses to allow them to forage in the meadow. The animals always came first.

Then we could eat. Leo would prepare dinner, usually fried steak and potatoes. Good too! By nine or ten p.m., I would crawl into my sleeping bag and sleep soundly until the horses decided to run through camp, their hobbled forelegs pounding the ground together – *thump, thump, thump.* I recall a silent prayer, *Please, please don't run over me.* That event happened at several camps and was some version of horseplay I suspect.

An ex-Navy Seabee with a can-do attitude, Leo worked long hours and held strong convictions on how to do things right, from the proper way to tie your horse's lead rope (never the reins) to a tree, or to build and maintain a trail. You knew you had his approval when he said, "You have earned the Navy's highest award – well done!"

Leo retired on the Inyo. At his retirement party Jack and Bruce wanted to present him with his favorite horse, Charlie, as a retirement gift. But how to do that? Charlie was, after all, 'Government property'. However, Charlie was getting older also and ready for retirement, which for a horse or mule often meant a trip to the glue factory. Jack figured out a way to consign the horse to the factory but buy him back privately.

Almost everyone on the forest showed up for the party in Bishop. They all knew and respected Leo. As the time came for the presentation of gifts, Bruce brought in a long rope that stretched all the way across the room from a side entrance. He presented it to Leo and said, "Here is your gift from the forest." I will never forget the look of confusion and anticipation on Leo's face. He felt a little tug on the rope, and while staring intently at the door fifty or more feet away, began to slowly pull it in. Soon Charlie appeared at the door, eyes wide and nostrils flared, but Hal Hunter held the horse in check. Leo, with tears streaming down his cheeks, slowly pulled Charlie into the room. It was a fitting ending for a good retirement party and Leo's great career.

Leo died a few years ago in Bishop, preceded by his wife, Areta.

The Lolo National Forest, Missoula, Montana 1974-1976

In the fall of 1974, I was offered a lateral transfer (no promotion) to Missoula, Montana as deputy forest supervisor on the Lolo National Forest. Everett had worked hard to arrange this placement for me. A deputy position was an expected and necessary step towards a forest supervisor position. At the time, achieving forest supervisor was both mysterious and difficult. The climate was very competitive, and I knew I had to avail myself of the opportunity of this 'stepping stone'.

No one else in the family really wanted to leave Bishop. It had been a great place to live. I pushed the issue, selfishly I admit, because I really wanted to be a forest supervisor and a deputy position was a step closer. So, for better or worse, we moved to Missoula, Montana.

In 1974 folks in Montana did not appreciate folks from California. Bumper stickers proclaimed, – "Don't Californicate Montana". Even clerks in the supermarkets reflected that attitude. Kaye wasn't excited about the move in the first place, and certainly this didn't help. Missoula was a full service city (the largest we had lived in to date) and had a good school system, plus the added benefit of the nearby University of Montana. It was the cultural center of Western Montana, and a pleasant, small city. We purchased a nice home on a hillside with a view of the city. I was hoping the upscale home and view would help Kaye and the kids feel a little better about the move and make amends for insisting on the transfer.

We moved there in the fall, and on Halloween we received our first snowfall! Missoula had a beautiful but very short summer. The kids and I enjoyed going to the college basketball and football games.

The previous forest supervisor and his deputy had both moved on to other assignments. Thus I was both the acting forest supervisor and the new deputy. I realized I was just holding the fort until the new supervisor arrived, but the situation went on for a couple of months, and I found I liked being the boss. And after all, a deputy was just one short step away from the forest supervisor's position I coveted.

Eventually a new forest supervisor was named, Orville Daniels from the Bitterroot National Forest located just to the south. The Bitterroot had gained national attention, along with the Monongahela National Forest in the east, over the growing issue of clear-cutting timber. There was an active environmental community in Missoula and the Bitterroot Valley.

Early on Orville told me he wanted to reorganize the forest in the format he developed on the Bitterroot, which did not include a deputy position. Suddenly I was to become the forest resource coordinator, a staff position without line authority. It was a hard pill to swallow. I had moved the family, changed from Region 5 to Region 1, all for the opportunity to be a deputy, and then it was gone. It was hard for both Kaye and I not to feel some bitterness about it, but I was determined to make the best of it.

I believe I was well accepted by the rest of the staff and district rangers, and I worked well with Orville. It was his watch over the forest, and I was duty-bound to help him run the forest his way. The regional forester, directors, and the 'culture' were another story.

Based on my experiences at Big Bear and on the Inyo, I believed the public's attitude toward timber harvest was evolving in favor of a more light-handed timber management approach, with a growing preference for preservation. The trend that I had observed and experienced in California was not a popular scenario to discuss in Montana in 1974.

A case in point: A timber sale purchaser had defaulted on his contract to harvest trees in the upper reaches of Welcome Creek, a major tributary to Rock Creek which was a renowned 'blue ribbon' trout stream east of Missoula. The regional office wanted the forest to again advertise and sell the sale. I researched the history of the sale and visited the site, accompanied by the forest's wildlife biologist. It seemed the dense stands of small diameter lodgepole pine were important, if not critical, thermal cover (shade) for elk in summer, and protection from the cold in winter. This, coupled with the importance of the drainage contributing clean, cool water to the high-profile Rock Creek, argued that we take a closer look at the wisdom of going forward with this sale.

Local environmentalists had Welcome Creek high on their list of areas to be set-aside in some kind of preservation status. I concluded that if we forced the issue of the sale, we would stimulate a strong response and possible political action from these groups. Some habitat manipulation (careful and selective tree harvest) to improve elk summer range could be a future option. For that reason I did not favor a legislated, preservation classification such as a 'Wilderness', but I also concluded the economic viability of the sale was questionable – witness the default of the original purchaser.

I recommended to the forest supervisor we not go forward with the timber sale as configured, but take a step back and redesign it as an elk habitat improvement project. Orville gave me the opportunity to make the case for withdrawing the sale from our program. On a subsequent field trip with the regional forester, a hard-nosed ex-marine officer and his stern director of timber management, I planned to do so.

I drove the sedan, and we were deep in the forest on a winding dirt road, a plume of dust chasing behind us. The regional forester was riding 'shotgun', and Orville and the director of timber management were in the backseat. I planned to bring up Welcome Creek and make my case, and I was a bit nervous.

The regional forester (RF), obviously a bit agitated, said, "You're driving a little fast, Ron, slow down!" I probably was driving faster than I should on those dirt roads, thinking more about what I wanted to say than paying attention to my driving. *Not a good beginning*, I thought.

I finally spoke up. "I've been reviewing the Welcome Creek Sale, and it appears to me the drainage is more important for elk habitat than timber production. Besides, the dense stands of small diameter trees are economically marginal to harvest. I recommend we hold off putting this sale up for auction again. We would like the opportunity to redesign it."

There was a long, uncomfortable silence.

I pressed on and summarized my analysis and conclusions by saying, "If we persist with this sale, I believe we just might push the environmental community into a political campaign to get the area classified as wilderness." I quickly added, "I do not believe wilderness is an appropriate designation for the area, as it would preclude elk habitat improvement projects."

My analysis and recommendations were met with more stony silence. *Well, I've put my foot in my mouth now*, I thought.

The director of timber management said at last, "The local timber industry is counting on the forest to re-offer this sale quickly, and commitments have been made."

The RF turned to Orville and curtly directed, "I want you to get this sale re-advertised and sold as quickly as possible." End of discussion, and lesson number two concerning the timber imperative received.

A couple of years later, under the sponsorship of then congressman now Senator Max Bacus, Welcome Creek was added to the National Wilderness Preservation System.

I did enjoy the hunting in Montana. Gordon Haugen, the forest fisheries biologist, and I made several trips to Eastern Montana to hunt ducks, deer, pheasant and sharp-tail grouse. The hunting was terrific. Mike and I hunted elk locally around Missoula, tracking them in fresh snow.

In the fall of 1976, I was offered a lateral transfer to Baker

City, Oregon to lead a planning team to develop a management plan for the newly created Hells Canyon National Recreation Area (HCNRA).

Remember the lateral transfer from Mad River to Big Bear years earlier in my career?

I initially turned this offer down, explaining to Orville this appeared to be a sidestep, and not a move forward toward my career goal of forest supervisor.

A few days later Orville came into my office and said, "The regional forester called and wants to speak with you about the Hells Canyon job."

"Damn! When?"

"First thing tomorrow morning."

I spent a restless night.

I entered the regional forester's office and found him behind his desk with a serious look on his somber face. He motioned to a chair in front of his desk, and I sat down. He explained to me that Region Six (the Pacific Northwest Region) really wanted me for this job, and in measured tones he suggested I accept it.

I recall thinking, *How could this be?* I didn't think I knew anyone in Region Six, and especially anyone who might have singled me out for this job. The regional forester did not counsel me about my career, or my ambitions, nor offer any encouragement to stay. Message received and understood; we were on our way to Oregon.

Ron McCormick Named to Succeed Gulick as Big Bear District Ranger

Ronald J. McCormick, assistant district ranger of the Big Bear District, U.S. Forest Service, has been promoted and named to succeed Miles Gulick as district ranger, it was announced by Donald R. Bauer, forest supervisor of the San Bernardino National Forest.

Gulick was recently promoted and transferred to the Sierra National Forest as district ranger of the Kings River District.

McCormick was born in Ohio, attended Ohio State University, and was graduated from the University of Michigan with a degree in forestry. He served a hitch in the U. S. Marine Corps, then began his Forest Service career in Idaho in 1954 He subsequently worked in California and the Six Rivers National Forest. He was transferred to the Big Bear District of the San Bernardino National Forest in October 1962 as assistant ranger.

Supervisor Bauer stated that McCormick's experience has encompassed all phases of multiple use management, including forest recreation, wildlife, timber and watershed management, range management, and fire prevention and control. He added that McCormick was well qualified to administer the valuable resources of the Big Bear District.

McCormick, his wife Kaye, their son Mike, 1½, and daughter Shannon, 3½, will move into the district ranger's quarters overlooking the Big Bear Ranger Station in late October.

RONALD McCORMICK

Shannon, Mike and I with Forest Service pickup, Big Bear Ranger Station

The John Muir Wilderness, Inyo National Forest

*Ron, Kaye, Shannon
and Mike*

*Danny and his tricycle,
Bishop, California*

Ranger Ron and his staff

Don Bauer and his rangers, San Bernardino NF

Supervisor, staff and district rangers, Inyo National Forest

CHAPTER FIVE

The Hells Canyon National Recreation Area

This period was one of the most eventful and difficult, yet in the end oddly fulfilling, in my life and career. The entire family experienced change and trauma during this chapter in our lives.

Hells Canyon of the Snake River is located in the extreme northeast corner of Oregon along the Oregon and Idaho border – it is very remote. I was to be the team leader of a planning team located in Baker, Oregon, the headquarters of the Wallowa-Whitman National Forest, called the W bar W (W-W) by employees. In the spring of 1976, I requested a couple of days off to drive to Baker (the community later reverted to the original and historic name of Baker City) to look the town over and check on available housing. Mike was also interested in what this new area and town were like, so he accompanied me.

We took the back way to Baker using secondary roads via Lewiston, Idaho and Joseph, Oregon. As we topped the last rise before dropping down into the small town of Joseph, the panorama of the snow-capped Wallowa Mountains as backdrop to the postcard perfect green valley of Wallowa spread out before us. It was a spectacular, breathtaking scene!

To the west was the hazy outline of the north rim of Hells Canyon. I knew I would soon be in contact with the good people of Joseph and Enterprise in the Wallowa Valley.

We drove through Joseph and Enterprise and in two more hours arrived in Baker.

Baker City

Baker City, Oregon was, and remains, a town of about ten thousand hardy people. At the time it was the center of the local ranching and logging industry. A local sawmill was the largest employer. Although not as striking as the Wallowa Valley, the setting was also picturesque – a valley enclosed by the Elkhorn Mountains to the west and the Wallowa Mountains to the northeast. The town itself was plain, and appeared a little worn and tired. It was a hardworking town of ranchers, loggers, and the businesses that served them. At an elevation of three thousand feet, the valley could have cold, snowbound winters. The number of houses for sale could be counted on one hand – not good news.

Mike and I checked out the few available houses for sale and didn't find anything we liked. We had enjoyed a very nice home in Missoula, and I resisted stepping down to something less. I was also hoping to locate a home on a few acres and thought that might be possible in the Baker Valley.

I left my name and phone number with a local realtor and asked him to call me if something came on the market he thought might work for my family. In the meantime, I rented two adjoining rooms with a kitchenette in a small, older motel in town, and we decided to make do there until a home came on the market. It was cramped and dismal, a real comedown from the beautiful home in Missoula. However, the kids were troopers and were to suffer the inconvenience without too much grumbling.

So we moved to Baker, leaving our furniture in the Missoula house until it sold.

Finally, after a month or so of struggling in the cramped quarters of the old motel, a nice ranch style, three-bedroom house, located outside of town, came available. We bought it. The house was situated on five pine-covered acres at the base of the Elkhorn Mountains with an irrigation ditch (more like a small creek) running through it. All in all it was quite nice, and we considered ourselves fortunate.

In the meantime, the Missoula house finally sold, and we moved into our new home in the Baker Valley. Within a year we added a fourth bedroom and installed a wood stove. Again, Kaye and I did all the work ourselves.

We soon acquired two dogs. One, Jody, a border collie cross, was a companion for the kids, and the other, a Brittany spaniel, I wanted for pheasant and chukar hunting, which the Baker Valley offered. We named the Brittany Prince, short for his registered name of Powder River Prince. He turned out to be a good pointer and retriever. I enjoyed hunting with him, often joined by Mike and Dan, and several times with Dad when he came to visit from Southern California.

Hunting excursions in wheat stubble fields on brisk, sunny, October mornings, under the backdrop of the Elkhorn Mountains, were golden moments that I treasure. Hunting with Dad made it extra special.

The Task

I began to realize I had accepted an enormous job. The size and scope seemed to grow. The key requirements of the seven-page act of December 31, 1975 that created the 653,000 acre Hells Canyon National Recreation Area (HCNRA) were sure to be hugely controversial and emotional 'hot buttons' in the region, and perhaps nationally.

The key purpose of the HCNRA Act was to prevent the construction of additional dams on the Snake River and keep it a free-flowing wild river. Other purposes were to protect fish and wildlife habitat, inventory the multitude of archeological and historic sites in the canyon and protect and interpret them; allow, but carefully manage traditional activities, i.e. cattle and sheep grazing, outfitter-guide operations; allow timber harvest by 'selective cutting', and develop regulations governing the use of private lands within the NRA.

A former employee of the W-W Forest, Wade Hall, was instrumental over the years in bringing national attention to 'America's deepest canyon' and stimulating the creation of the National Recreation Area. Wade was retired, lived in Baker and was still active in matters concerning the canyon. He would prove to be a good information resource.

The requirements of the HCNRA Act were many and each complex in their own right. We were charged with the task to:

> *Develop and submit to Congress within 5 years of the Act becoming law an HCNRA Comprehensive Management Plan. Establish and publish the boundaries of the HCNRA and the Wild and Scenic River. Study three designated areas for possible Wilderness classification. Acquire private in-holdings as deemed desirable. Promulgate rules and regulations for the use and development of the remaining private lands within the HCNRA. And set limits and control the use and number of motorized (jet boat) and non-motorized river craft (rafts) using the river.*

I arrived less than a year after the HCNRA Act was signed into law and discovered there was not yet a planning organization in place, save Greg McClarren, who was already on the forest and had been reassigned to do the wilderness evaluation on the HCNRA. I was most alarmed to discover there was no budget in place to finance a team and no prospect for getting the funds. And the clock was ticking.

To cap it off, the newly created HCNRA was an administrative nightmare. It straddled the major geographic and political divide of the Snake River, and the enormous Hells Canyon it traversed. The HCNRA included parts of three states – Oregon, Idaho and

Washington; three regions of the Forest Service – Regions One, Four and Six; three national forests – the Wallowa-Whitman, Nez Perce, and Payette; and four counties. It had not been made clear who had the lead, and there was no administrative unit established. Out of necessity and by default, the task of getting a unit established fell into the lap of the planning team.

I quickly decided that as a first order of business I had to get the funds needed to bring on some help. I needed people experienced in recreation planning, land acquisition, wildlife management, and archeology. The Wallowa-Whitman Forest did not have the funds, nor did the regional office in Portland.

One evening I read in the local paper that Oregon Congressman Al Ullman was going to visit Baker City. I learned he had been one of the prime movers in writing the HCNRA legislation. However, it was not appropriate for a mid-level Forest Service person to contact a congressman directly to request funding. A federal employee just did not 'end run' the budgeting process, and there were consequences for doing so.

I learned that Congressman Ullman was staying that night at a local motel. I took a chance and called the motel. The switchboard rang his room, and to my great surprise he answered! I had fully expected to be intercepted by a secretary or staff person.

I explained the situation to Mr. Ullman, and emphasized that I was eager to get the planning team assembled and get started on the Comprehensive Management Plan (CMP) in order to meet the date prescribed by the law. He was cordial and receptive but seemed surprised to learn of the absence of funding. He asked me how much I needed, and I told him. He said he would look into it. Not long afterward the funds showed up, earmarked for HCNRA planning, which included funds for the following year also. Regional and forest officials were surprised. I never told anyone how the funds were secured.

I developed vacancy announcements for the positions I needed and had them circulated nationwide. In due time we had Jim Hulbert, Dave Odahl, Frank Hunsaker, John Baglien, Janet Friedman, and Don Bush on the team, and we were ready to go. Paula Bowling and her personnel department on the W-W were very responsive and of great help to me in quickly getting a team on board.

The Process

The months that followed were a blur of meetings with interest groups from around the HCNRA. I traveled to Enterprise and Joseph in Oregon, and Lewiston, Riggins and Boise in Idaho. My plan was to educate our publics on the intent and requirements of the act that created the HCNRA and to listen to their views on the key issues they wanted the planning team to address in order to produce a viable CMP. I wanted to develop the plan with the full participation of the interest groups that comprised our publics. I wanted their support when we submitted the CMP to the Secretary of Agriculture, as was required for approval.

The Imnaha River is a major tributary to the Snake River. It is a narrow canyon, more of a gorge actually, with small, rolling flats along the river. Much of the land along the Imnaha is private and subject to the federal government (the team) developing and implementing regulations and establishing 'standards for the use and development of privately owned property within the recreation area.' Driving down into the Imnaha canyon was to go back in time to the early 1900s. The only service facility was the Imnaha Store and gas station, where the paved access road terminated in the bottom of the canyon.

Up and down the canyon along a gravel road were small, rural ranches scattered along the river.

These were homesteads occupied by a group of close-knit, self-reliant, and fiercely independent people. Some had been there for fifty years or more, and some were second generation. I couldn't help but respect and even admire these pioneers. One can imagine just how distasteful the notion was that the federal government was going to tell them what they could and could not do with their land. They hated the idea, did not trust the federal government, and resented the representative that brought the message – me.

We held several meetings at the local grange hall, several miles upstream from the Imnaha Store. They were usually held in the evening, and we would have a full house of fifty or more locals. Most of the ranchers were courteous and respectful, but a little distant.

At one of these sessions I noticed a large, rawboned rancher sitting in the back of the room. He sat quietly, wringing his powerful, work-scarred hands and staring at the floor. I was up front answering questions after my presentation. My eyes would frequently wander to him. He never looked up, and I had a premonition.

I found out later the man's name was Lyman Goucher. He had moved there from the Central California coast a few years previous when the state bought up land for a park. He thought he had moved as far away from government intervention as he could get. You can just imagine his frustration and anger.

Near the end of the meeting, Mr. Goucher stood up and strode up the aisle, his face contorted in anger, and his fists were clenched. I knew I was going to get hit and was trying to decide how to react. At the last moment Gladys Marks, the grange master, stood up between us. Mrs. Marks was in her mid-seventies, five feet tall, and weighed perhaps ninety-five pounds.

She looked up and stared directly into Mr. Goucher's eyes, shook her finger and said, "Lyman Goucher, there will be no violence in my grange hall."

He looked down at her sheepishly and said, "Yes, ma'am," and stomped out the door and into the darkness.

She had saved me from a beating, and who knows what else. I

heard the door to his pickup slam shut, but I didn't hear him leave. I summarized quickly and concluded the meeting, fully aware of a crawling, itching sensation up and down my back. The recollection and image of rifles slung across the gun racks in the back window of nearly every pickup in the parking lot dominated my mind. I couldn't think of anything else but to get out of there.

We soon realized that imposing the heavy hand of the federal government on these people in dictating the use of their land was not only inappropriate, but it just would not work. The purpose of the regulations was to perpetuate the rural nature of the ranches of the Imnaha, which the local residents also wanted. Therefore, based on a suggestion from Tom Kovalicky of Region 1, we drafted the necessary language in the form of supplementary provisions and negotiated with Wallow County officials to add these provisions to their existing county ordinances. It was a compromise, but a good one, and I felt it met the intent of the HCNRA Act.

Dark Clouds

In July of 1977, I returned home from a series of meetings in Portland – I believe I had been gone nearly a week – and Kaye said we needed to talk. We walked into the backyard and into the woods along the creek. She told me she was leaving me. I never fully understood the reasons, but some had to do with the Forest Service – I was absent a lot. And I suppose I was not the easiest person to live with, especially during that period. Six months later we were divorced. This was a very difficult period for everyone, but especially Shannon, Mike and Dan, and I feel badly about it to this day.

In August of 1978, in response to some criticism I received from Forest Supervisor Oard about the amount of traveling I was doing, I prepared a summary of formal meetings, presentations and significant special interest group contacts I had made since July of 1976 and presented it to Supervisor Oard.

There were seventy-seven major contacts with groups and organizations that included the chambers of commerce of all the surrounding towns, Rotary and Lions Clubs, university professors, Isaac Walton League, Oregon and Idaho State Fish and Wildlife officials, Oregon and Idaho Outfitter Guides, Nez Perce and Umatilla Indian Tribal Councils, County Commissioners of five counties in three states, senators and congressmen and their staff people, Hells Canyon Preservation Council, Imnaha Grange, National Marine Fisheries Service, and Forest Service officials in Washington, D.C.

Some of these meetings and presentations were at their invitation, some I initiated, and many we met with more than once. I knew, and insisted, that we had to get understanding and acceptance of the reality that the HCNRA had been established, and that there was going to be a management plan, and most importantly that we intended to engage the public in developing it. I didn't hear anything more about 'excessive travel' from Forest Supervisor Oard.

My relationship with Al Oard was contentious. He had really preferred to handle the HCNRA planning with his then existing staff and had not wanted a planning team leader and team assigned to his forest. The Washington and regional offices had imposed that on him. Square-jawed with a gray crew cut, he was a tough, determined man who had flown bombers during World War II.

We had several face-to-face confrontations. One day we were literally nose-to-nose when he said, "I don't need you here, I don't want you here, and I'm going to run you off this forest."

I stood my ground and said, "Al, I don't run easily; you'd better pack a big lunch because it's going to be a battle."

We were still face-to-face, about three inches apart. I saw the corner of his mouth crack into a tiny smile. I was to learn that he respected 'backbone'. If you stood up to him, he would at least tolerate you. In time we developed a wary but respectful relationship. In some ways I grew to admire him.

A Wilderness Backpack

I also made time to leave the office and meetings to 'get on the ground'. I wanted to learn as much as I could firsthand about the geography and natural resources of the HCNRA, their condition and trend, and public use patterns. That part of the job I loved: Driving the existing back roads, rafting or jet boating the Snake River, hiking, and sometimes backpacking the more remote areas. If it weren't for those brief interludes, this job would have made me crazy.

On the Idaho side of the Snake River, and within the Payette National Forest, the imposing Seven Devils Mountains and Wilderness dominated the skyline. I felt some of the team members and I needed to see and be familiar with this area because part of our task was to develop wilderness management guidelines. I set up a backpack trip and asked Tom Kovalicky, the wilderness specialist from Region 1 in Missoula, to join us and be our guide.

Since my job took me away from home a lot, I missed out on many of the kids' activities, so I asked my son Mike to join us on this adventure. He was about fourteen at the time and school was out for the summer. It was a several-day backpack trip that made a large circle around the primary peaks of the Seven Devils Mountains. The weather was warm, even at the six-thousand-foot-plus elevations, and we made a long day's march each day and slept out in the open. Kovalicky was a practical joker, and each morning he managed to covertly slip a large rock into the pack of one of the team members. The rock was usually discovered at the end of that day's trek and was always good for a laugh.

At the end of the trip, as we were breaking down our packs, Mike discovered a five-pound rock that had been surreptitiously stashed in the very bottom of his pack. He just stared at the rock, a mixture of shock and puzzlement on his face. Kovalicky was doubled over in laughter. Mike had carried that rock up and down hills for several days and for over fifty miles! Mike has never forgotten that trip and has always asked me about Kovalicky. A few years later Tom went on to become the forest supervisor of the Nez Perce National Forest in Idaho.

Rapids and Bears

I also managed to participate in a few raft trips down the Snake River, which fired my interest in river rafting – an interest that has persisted to this day. In May 1978, I asked the forest's procurement personnel to find me a good outfitter-guide and to set up a trip down the river for several Forest Service officials and others who would be influential as our planning took form. This included, among others, Deputy Regional Forester Jim Torrence, David Lime from the Forest Service research arm, and Jim Snow, an attorney for the Office of General Counsel in Washington, D.C.

I did not get the outfitter I wanted, one I knew to be competent. The forest's procurement people insisted I take the lowest bidder. It was an outfit I was not familiar with, and I objected, but was overruled. The Snake River flows were predicted to be about normal at 18,000 CFS (cubic feet per second), and some showers or light rain was forecast. The first day went OK under cloudy skies. At the first night's camp, just above the largest rapid in the river, named Granite Falls, it began to rain. It rained steadily and hard all night. In the morning at first light, we hiked down a trail carved into the face of a cliff to scout Granite Falls Rapids. The river had risen alarmingly and was a menacing, chocolate-colored torrent. Idaho Power, who operated the Hells Canyon dam immediately upriver, was apparently releasing an unusual amount of water in anticipation of a large storm. Later we learned the river was running at 45,000 CFS – a dangerous torrent of powerful water almost three times the normal flow.

That morning the head outfitter and his boatman were both

sick. Apparently they had sat in their tent and drank whiskey all night. They were throwing up and moaning. Clearly they were in no condition to be at the oars of our two rafts. In fact, they refused. *Oh, the lowest bidders*, I thought.

Jim Hulbert agreed to row one raft, and I took the other. It was cold and raining steadily. I recall that going down the 'tongue' of Granite Rapids was a bit like that first, spine-tingling descent on a roller coaster. It was a deceptively smooth, but huge and steep drop. At the end of the initial drop, it abruptly bottomed and rose up in a steep wall of water – called a standing wave – twenty feet high.

Jim went first. His raft descended into the trough then climbed the wave, the bow pointed skyward, hesitated at the top then plunged down the other side. It vanished from my view. *That doesn't look too bad*, I thought.

I was close behind, and it appeared I was lined up OK. We accelerated down the tongue into the trough then abruptly climbed out and clawed our way up this mountain of a wave. Events can happen quickly in the middle of a raging river rapid. As we crested the top of the wave the blade of my right oar caught the back-curl of the wave, and it ripped the oar from my hand. That turned us a little sideways, so we crested the top a little 'out of shape'. Being a bit sideways combined with the jolt of slamming down over the top catapulted both me and Jim Snow out of the raft. I came to the surface after what seemed a long time. My head bumped the bottom of the raft; I was directly under it! In the muddy water I could feel the raft but not see it. I felt my way to the edge and popped to the surface.

We were fortunate that the raft had not flipped over. I could see Jim Torrence and David Lime hanging on. With their help I was able to clamor back into the raft and again took the oars. I looked for Jim Snow. He was already down the river a hundred yards, and Hulbert was rowing hard trying to catch up with him. Hulbert soon reached him and pulled the near helpless man into the raft. Jim

Snow was cold and could hardly move. He had been in the water twenty minutes or more and exhibited the first symptoms of hypothermia. I pulled along side and we rowed to shore and built a fire under the shelter of a rock ledge – an old Indian cliff shelter actually. Snow was shaking uncontrollably, and I could hear his teeth chattering. We retrieved dry clothes from his gear bag and helped him change. He eventually warmed up. I was also wet and cold, but not near as bad as Jim Snow. I changed clothes and soon warmed up as well.

Hulbert and I finished the trip that day with no problems, successfully running several more rapids at flood stage. This was a memorable trip for all involved, and especially for Jim Snow and me.

In a subsequent raft trip on the Snake, this time with a competent outfitter, we made the first night's camp at the same location above Granite Falls Rapids. I had invited Ted Yarosh, the deputy forest supervisor of the Wallowa-Whitman, and several of the key office staff. My objective was to provide them with an understanding of the issues we were addressing regarding river management and archeological site protection and interpretation.

We had spotted a cinnamon-colored black bear as we made camp. It prowled around the perimeter of the campsite. That night we carefully cleaned the camp of food scraps and put the ice chests in the rafts and tied them off so they remained off shore, making it difficult for a bear to reach. About midnight there was a commotion, and I arose from my sleeping bag to find that Don Busch, our team illustrator and photographer, was bleeding from his scalp. We guessed that a pinecone or branch had fallen from the tree above and struck his head. We were not using tents.

About two in the morning I heard a scream beside me. I looked over to see that the bear had clamped onto the thigh of Ted's right leg through the sleeping bag. I sat up and yelled. The bear reared up, still holding onto Ted. I thought I could see Ted hitting the bear in the side with his fist. I grabbed a nearby rock to throw, but the bear had let go and backed off a few feet, staring at me. By that time the whole camp was up and yelling and screaming, and the bear retreated into the woods. No one went back to bed that night. We built up the fire, huddled together, and listened to the bear growl, grunt and prowl around and around the camp for the rest of the night, thrashing through bushes just outside the circle of campfire light.

In the morning we called in a helicopter via a portable radio, and Ted and Don were flown out for treatment and observation. The uncharacteristic behavior of that bear led doctors to suspect the bear might be rabid. The rest of us proceeded down the river. An Idaho Fish and Wildlife warden was called in and he shot the bear, which was found not to be rabid.

The next night at camp I put up a tent. Greg and I were going to share it, but it was hot so we decided to sleep out under the stars. I finally went to sleep, only to have a mouse or small critter scamper over my sleeping bag. I awoke with a start and decided to get into the tent. It just felt safer!

Ted was the star attraction in the office for several weeks to follow. He would tell the bear attack story and offer to show folks where it bit him high on his thigh. Pulling down his trousers the ladies would often turn away, only to find he was wearing swim trunks!

The Clouds Part

In 1977, a clerk in administrative services brought an attractive young woman around to the various departments and introduced her as the new mail clerk. She and her two young children, Todd and Trina, had recently moved to Baker from Klamath Falls, Oregon. I later learned that she was divorced. Her name was Carol Worlein. She had long dark hair, soft brown eyes and a gentle demeanor. I was struck by her beauty and wonderful smile. I recall that first brief introduction feeling like a ray of sunshine had just brightened my life.

I was to eventually learn that she was as lovely on the inside as she was outside. The term 'smitten' seems appropriate, but it took me until January 1978 to ask her on a date. We went to lunch on January 13, 1978. It was on a Friday, as I recall, and we walked over to the restaurant at the old Baker Hotel. About a third of the office personnel were in there having lunch. I am sure we became a favorite topic of office conversation and speculation over the next few months.

On November 24, 1979, Carol and I were married in the Methodist Church in Baker City. Her two children, Todd and Trina, plus my children, Dan, Shannon and Mike, had a role in the wedding. Both her parents and mine were able to attend. A large number of our Forest Service friends and co-workers were also present. In some ways it seemed a union sanctioned and blessed by both our natural families and our Forest Service family.

The Draft Comprehensive Management Plan

I have dwelled on some of the highlights of our planning process. The facts are that it was an enormous and difficult task. There were so many facets and steps to the multiple tasks the team was charged to complete that I made a multi-year flow chart to help keep myself and the team on track. I tacked it to a small bulletin board above my desk in order to visually monitor our progress.

I was determined to meet the dates prescribed by the HCNRA Act. To stay on track we needed to have the draft CMP and Draft Environmental Impact Statement (DEIS) to the public by fall 1979.

I knew we needed a writer/editor to help us pull the plan and DEIS together into a polished, professional document. I learned that a person with those credentials happened to be in Baker City and was looking for work. I interviewed him and learned he had done work for the Oregonian newspaper, and documentaries for a

Portland TV station. His work looked good so I hired him. Jack Berry turned out to be an excellent editor and writer and became a valued team member.

We published and released the DEIS on November 13, 1979. I have kept a copy and reviewed it while writing this portion of my memoirs. We set an ambitious schedule for ourselves and worked long days. We produced, with the involvement and help of our publics, a sound plan and DEIS. The credit for this accomplishment belongs to planning team stalwarts Jim Hulbert, Greg McClarren, Dave Odahl, Jan Friedman, John Baglien, Don Busch and Jack Berry. We did a great job!

The only person to say 'well done' was Tony Skufca, director of recreation in the regional office.

Public Law 94-199 was signed on December 31, 1975 establishing the HCNRA. Most of our work was accomplished during the Carter administration of 1977-1981. The DEIS was produced during this time.

Following an election and a change in administrations, President Reagan and his Republican administration were in place when the final plan and Final Environmental Impact Statement (FEIS) were about to be published. In the meantime, Senator McClure of Idaho had evolved into a powerful and influential senator, and John Crowell had replaced Rupert Cutler as Assistant Secretary of Agriculture. Mr. Cutler came from a position as assistant professor of resource development at Michigan State University. Before that he had been executive director of the Wilderness Society. Mr. Crowell came from the Louisiana Pacific Lumber Company and had been their chief counsel, before that he worked for Georgia Pacific Lumber Company.

Both were fine men in their own right but worlds apart in their views of natural resource protection and management.

The term 'transition' is used to describe the changing of administrations. That implies a handoff, as in a relay, of the baton of responsibility from the present runner to a new and fresh runner heading in the same direction. In my experience that image is flawed. The handoff is more often to someone going in an entirely different direction and collisions are likely!

Thus, the HCNRA bill was conceived and passed during a Democratic administration, and the planning had taken place in the context of a Democratic administration. However, the final plan and FEIS would be reviewed and approved by a Republican administration. The rules of the game had clearly changed, and I was worried.

The DEIS was released to the public on November 13, 1979. Carol and I were married on November 24. I was promoted to assistant director of recreation for Region Six at about the same time, and Carol, Todd, Trina and I moved to Portland, Oregon in late December 1979. I was busy with meetings and presentations on the DEIS right up until the time we left Baker City.

I wasn't finished and really didn't want to leave just yet. But the assistant director position had been created by Director of Recreation Tony Skufca with me in mind, and I was obligated to accept it. I left the project in the capable hands of Jim Hulbert and the rest of the team. I took some comfort from that, and the knowledge that in my new position I would still be involved with the Hells Canyon NRA.

We left Baker City the same day the moving van left for Portland. It was snowing, and a big storm was predicted. We decided not to travel I-5 through the Columbia River Gorge but follow the back roads through the mountains to Portland. I drove my little Ford Courier pickup, and Carol her Ford Pinto wagon. We traveled on snow-packed highways most of the way, and we arrived at our new home well after dark.

We learned the Columbia River Gorge and Interstate 5 were experiencing blizzard conditions. The moving van became snowbound on I-5 somewhere in the Columbia Gorge. Therefore, we didn't have furniture or bedding. I was a veteran of many Forest Service moves, and we had packed some emergency supplies. We camped out in the house with sleeping bags and used camp cook gear to subsist in our new home at Rock Creek, west of Portland. The kids looked at it as a big adventure. The moving van finally showed up several days later. Within a few days Carol and I began our new assignments in the regional office in downtown Portland.

Back in Baker City, Jim Hulbert and Greg McClarren stayed on to put the final CMP and FEIS together. In the draft plan we had established a permit system for both rafts and powerboats on the Snake River, set dates for a regulated river season, and limits on both the number of raft launches and powerboat trips upriver. With the change in the political landscape, the powerboat folks convinced Senator McClure and Assistant Secretary Crowell to drop any regulation of powerboat use from the plan.

The restrictions and guidelines on timber harvest were also weakened. I was angry and disgusted. The team had devoted a great deal of time and effort to work out agreements with, and had won acceptance from, the various interest groups around the NRA. We knew we had achieved a near consensus on how to protect and manage the NRA. These agreements, earned over a couple of years of hard work with our various public interest groups, were all negated with a change in political party. The newly elected or appointed political positions in the new administration redeemed some political obligations by using a few strokes of a pen to emasculate this carefully constructed plan.

Lessons Learned

When the stakes are high, a lifestyle threatened or a great deal of money involved, public land and natural resource management decisions almost always become political decisions. In spite of the best intentions to forge consensus decisions through genuine public involvement and participation, the special interest group with the best political connections *at that point in time* will usually exploit their political opportunity and call in political debt. Ideology prevails, and there are winners and losers. In the political game our public lands and natural resources become pawns and often end up in the 'loss' column.

The Pacific Northwest Region, Portland, Oregon

There was genius in the organizational design of the newly created Forest Service in 1905.

The first chief of the Forest Service, Gifford Pinchot, determined that within the geographically far-flung system of national forests across the nation, local decisions would be made on local ground.

A hierarchical organization, with strong delegation of authority to the field, was established. District rangers, forest supervisors and regional foresters were line officers and had line authority. Everyone else was staff.

Configurations of regions and national forests evolved over time. As of this writing there are ten regions, and 155 national forests.

My new position in the Pacific Northwest Region, known as Region Six, was to be the staff position of 'Assistant Director for Outdoor Recreation'. The nineteen national forests of Oregon and Washington were in this region.

The director of recreation was Tony Skufca. He had been both a district ranger and forest supervisor, had completed a tour in the Washington office, and was knowledgeable and wise in how the organization functioned. Tony had been my principle regional office contact while I was doing the HCNRA plan. He would call me at my Baker City office occasionally and before he would even say hello, I would hear, "Have you got it done yet?" followed by a chuckle. He had a low-key, dry sense of humor. Tony was a pleasure to work for.

We did 'get it done', and my reward was a promotion to Portland and the regional office. Tony had seen to it that I was taken care of; and I was grateful, for it wasn't clear to me what my next move would be from the non-traditional planning position I occupied.

I took a deep breath. The conflict, turmoil and intensity of the HCNRA planning marathon were behind me, or at least I could be involved from a distance. That task, combined with the divorce from Kaye, had taken a huge toll. I was emotionally drained.

Regional offices were removed from the 'front lines', and the pace and intensity more measured. I realized this was a respite, and I knew I needed to recharge. However, the position of assistant director offered me a wider perspective of national forest issues, policy and budget. It afforded me an opportunity to learn and to grow.

Tony retired a couple of years later. During the interim, and before a new director was selected, I was named acting director. As such I was a principle staff to the deputy regional forester and regional forester. In that role I was involved in all major policy decisions, not only in outdoor recreation, for which I was expected to be the subject matter expert, but also in the full spectrum of resource and land management issues. I remained acting director for nearly a year.

After a couple of months I found I really liked that role. I decided to apply for the director position, knowing it would be a long shot, as I had not yet completed a tour in the Washington office. At the time that was an informal requirement and stepping stone before you could be selected for a director's position.

Dave Scott, then in the division of recreation in the Washington office, was selected. I was disappointed but not surprised. I knew Dave well from Region Five, California. He had been the recreation staff officer on the San Bernardino Forest when I was the district ranger at Big Bear. He was very competent and I liked him. Two good bosses in a row!

I had a good staff in Portland, a good boss, and I enjoyed the experience. I formed sound working relationships with the regional forester and deputies, and the other directors of the divisions of planning, timber management, range, fish and wildlife, lands and minerals, watershed, public information, and engineering. These relationships were to prove valuable in the future.

Kaye called me from Baker one evening to say that Dan was struggling in school a bit and was in need of some help and discipline. She wanted him to stay with us for a while. That was fine with me. I converted part of the downstairs family room to a forth bedroom for Dan, and I finished the bathroom down there that had been rough plumbed but never completed. Todd, Trina and Dan seemed to get along well, and it was nice to have Dan in our home.

Carol and I both worked with Dan to help him complete homework assignments, and this, combined with the excellent school system and teachers in the county, helped him improve his grades.

The downside was living in a big city environment. Portland is a great city, relatively speaking. I had always known I was not a city person. Time passed, and one cold December morning while standing in the dark, in the rain, waiting for a bus to commute to the city center, I knew this had to be temporary. It was time to apply for forest supervisor positions.

Incident at Blossom Bar

In the meantime, I wanted to get out of the city on weekends. I felt the entire family would benefit from an adventurous, outdoor diversion in which we could all participate. Perhaps rafting rivers!

Rivers have always fascinated me. I like to be on or near them. I fished and trapped them as a kid. In Montana my children, Shannon, Mike, Dan and I canoed the Bitterroot, Blackfoot and Clark's Fork Rivers. The kids enjoyed the outings, and I became pretty good at 'reading' whitewater. Later, during the Hells Canyon assignment, I had the occasion to raft the Snake River with an outfitter-guide, and that experience convinced me that at some point we would have an inflatable raft.

I discussed it with Carol. She said, "OK, as long as it is of good quality and safe." She was always good about going along with my dreams for adventure. I began reading the classified ads in the Oregonian newspaper for used rafts. I located a newer fourteen-foot raft, completely outfitted with an aluminum frame, plywood floor, a hand-operated bail pump mounted on the frame, cooler, and oars. Perfect! Carol and I went to see it. We inspected it closely and it appeared to be in good shape. I glanced at Carol, and she smiled and nodded. The owner was in the midst of an ugly divorce and sold it to us for a very reasonable price.

Our old yellow Ford Courier pickup had a canopy and a boat rack. The truck was underpowered but dependable. We figured out how to tie the aluminum frame to the boat rack, and then roll-up the rubber boat and stuff it in the bed of the pickup along with the two boys – Trina could fit in the small cab with us. Although cramped, no one seemed to mind. We were off on a river adventure!

We did some 'day floats' on the nearby Sandy and Clackamas Rivers, and an overnight trip on the John Day River. For that trip I borrowed a small two-man raft from Dale Farley, who also worked in the recreation division. This would provide the two boys with their own raft to row.

The children were eager participants, and together we learned how to pack and secure gear on the rafts, prepare meals and put up tents. The kids also learned the basics of rowing a raft. Todd, Dan and Trina really took to the adventure of an overnight river trip, and Carol loved it, partly because it involved the whole family doing it together, and partly because she genuinely liked being on rivers.

In early June of 1983, we had an opportunity to join a group making the three-day raft trip down the wild section of the Rogue River from Grave Creek to Foster Bar, about thirty-five miles of whitewater river. The Rogue was part of the nation's Wild and Scenic River system established by law. The Rogue flowed through the Siskiyou National Forest and adjoining BLM administered public lands. Our friend, Dale Farley, had been successful in drawing a coveted permit in the annual lottery conducted by the Forest Service, and he invited us to go along. We jumped at the chance.

Carol, Todd, Dan and I traveled to Grants Pass in our Ford Courier with our raft and camping gear. We made other arrangements for Trina, feeling she was a bit young yet for this level of whitewater trip. I knew she was disappointed and a little miffed. "I want to go," she said. "I rafted the John Day and I don't know why I can't go!"

However, Carol and I knew the Rogue was a much more difficult river than the John Day, and we remained firm she would have to pass this one up. In retrospect, we made a good decision. We stayed overnight at Motel 6. We were to meet our friends the next morning to launch on the river.

Dale was to be our trip leader and guide. He was a quiet, unassuming man that inspired confidence. He had previously worked on the Siskiyou and prepared the Rogue River Management Plan. He was the architect of the river permit and lottery system. He had rafted the Rogue many times. I felt we were in good hands.

Mary and Ted Stubblefield, his son Brett, John and Glenda Berry, and Dale and his wife, Judy, were going to be our river companions for three days. Ted and John both worked on the Siskiyou National Forest, so they and their families lived in the area. The weather was to be good on the day of our launch, but the forecast was ominous. We could have rain later the next day.

Launch day had finally arrived! We were on the river about

noon and it was warm and sunny. We were all excited and a little anxious but happy to finally be there. Dale held a brief river safety talk before we launched.

"Always wear your life vest in any riffle or rapid. If you fall out of the raft, float feet first to fend off rocks, and one of us will pick you up." He also mentioned we would stop and scout several major rapids we would encounter.

The first day met all our expectations and more. It was pleasantly warm, the river and scenery beautiful, the rapids exhilarating. We had successfully run Grave Creek Falls, the tricky bypass around Rainie Falls, and the class III Grave Creek, Tyee, and Wildcat Rapids. It had been exciting and fun, and we were all feeling pretty good about the day. That night we camped on a bench just above the river. We sat around a campfire and relived the day's adventures, and talked about tomorrow's challenges.

Ted related the story about his first trip down the Rogue the year before, and their passage through Blossom Bar Rapids. He was a passenger on that first trip. The day before a drift boat had overturned on the rocks at the entry to this infamous and dangerous rapid. The aluminum boat lay bottom side up, just below the surface, and partially blocked the entry. A recovery team was in place trying to extract a body from under the drift boat as their raft squeezed by. Ted said the body was clearly visible just under the surface. A gut wrenching and sobering sight!

Black Bar Falls and Mule Creek Rapids waited just downriver, then Blossom Bar, a technically difficult and dangerous class IV rapid. As Ted had reminded us, several people had drowned in this rapid over the years. I was apprehensive and did not sleep well that night. I was confident about my boatman skills, but something just did not feel right.

The weather in June can change quickly. One day it is summer, and the next can be a return to winter. At daybreak it was cloudy and cool. We had a quick breakfast, broke camp, packed up our gear in the rafts and launched. It began raining lightly by midmorning. On a raft, where you are wet anyway from the spray of the waves, it becomes impossible to stay warm in cool and rainy conditions. It just isn't fun to float down a river in a cold rain.

As we approached Blossom Bar Rapids we were all a little wet and cold. I was ready to get this over with. The procedure at Blossom Bar is to stop on the right side of the river just above the rapid, scramble along the rock cliffs to a point a hundred yards or so downriver to 'scout' the rapid and figure out the best route through. It is important to commit that route to memory.

We hiked to the vantage point to look down at the rapid from seventy-five feet or so above the river. The roar of the whitewater was intimidating. Looking down all I could see was a jumble of huge boulders and whitewater – a furious, swirling cauldron of rocks and whitewater. I thought I could see the line we needed to take through the rapid.

Ted exclaimed, "If we stay here and look any longer, I am going to throw up!"

Cold and anxious, I suddenly had to relieve myself and stepped behind a large rock. When I returned, the rest of the party was returning to the rafts. Carol told me they had the opportunity to watch another party in a raft pass safely through the rapid. I wished I could have watched how they did it.

Back at the boats, Ted fetched a roll of toilet paper from his raft's 'dry box', and disappeared behind a rock. I wasn't the only one that was apprehensive. Dale suggested that Dan ride with him and Judy. That would put three people in each boat, dividing up the weight a little better. I agreed. After studying the rapid and thinking about it, Glenda decided to walk around it and meet us at the bottom. We made one final check of our gear: *Is everything tied down securely? Spare oar in place and readily available? No loose lines or articles in the bottom of the raft? Life vests snug and fastened?* We were ready.

The key to negotiating this rapid safely is to first locate and then drop through a narrow slot or 'pour-off' between two boulders in the middle of the river. To do this, it is best to start on the extreme left side of the river with the bow of the raft inches away from the cliff face. As the speed of the current picks up, one must back ferry (row backwards) strongly with a slight downstream angle across the strong current towards the center of the river and above the dreaded 'Picket Fence', then pop into an eddy just ahead of the 'pour-off'. At that point you need to swing the raft to point downriver and shoot through a narrow slot between the rocks and down the rock free passage. From there on down it is just a matter of dodging huge boulders spaced inconveniently in the middle of the rapid until you reach calmer water a couple of hundred yards below.

The problem is the entry to the slot, and the pour-off is partially obscured, which is the main factor that makes this rapid tricky and dangerous. You cannot see this critical slot from upriver, as it is hidden by a large boulder. You can't see it until you are on top of it – you just have to know where it is, anticipate it and back ferry the raft across the current and into it. If you don't quite make it to the slot, to the left is a row of pointed rocks aptly named the 'Picket Fence', and you will be onto these rocks quickly and hard. There is not enough room to pass safely between them, and there is an enormous, boiling cauldron of whitewater around and below them. These rock have hung up many an unwary or inexperienced rafter or 'first timer'. Several boaters had, indeed, drowned there.

Dale rowed across the river to the cliff face on the left side, and John followed closely behind. John held back as Dale entered the quickening current and began to back ferry hard across the current to reach the eddy leading to the slot and pour-off. I held back to provide some maneuvering space, and when Dale pulled behind the boulder to begin his approach I tried to observe. I saw him move to the right, across the strong current, and disappear behind the large boulder that hid the pour-off.

Then John followed. I was too busy to see if he made it. I was back ferrying hard, my head cranked around over my shoulder, eyes searching for the boulder that hides the slot and pour-off. What looked so obvious from the scouting position above became more obscure at river level while rowing hard and backwards in a fast-moving current.

I hollered at Carol above the rapid's roar, "Help me find it, I don't see it!"

We were picking up speed in the strong current and headed toward the Picket Fence. There seemed to be more than one opening. I was momentarily confused, but I thought I saw it and yelled over the roar of the rapid just below us, "Carol is that it? Do you see it?"

She yelled, "Yes. There, there!" and pointed.

But I was a little late. I knew I wouldn't make it. My moment of hesitation cost us the few critical feet of river we needed to cross to get to the slot and pour-off, and the right side of the raft road up onto one of the Picket Fence rocks and the power of the rapid pinned us hard against the rock. The stern of the raft holding all our gear was forced underwater, and a torrent of river was pouring across the back half of the raft and up and over my lap. I was still sitting down trying to hold on to the oars. I shouted to Carol and Todd, "Get to the high side!" A maneuver we had rehearsed in case of just such an event that can shift the weight in the raft, allowing the rushing water to raise the buried side and lift us off the rock.

I watched in amazement as Carol scrambled over the bow of the raft and on to the rock. She perched precariously on its pointed top with whitewater crashing all around. *Why in hell did she climb up there?* The question flashed through my mind. With the bow and right side of the raft suddenly lighter, it began to move, and I shouted to Carol, "Get back in, we are moving!" She stepped back on the bow tube of the raft, but it was wet and slick and she slipped and fell into the rapid on the downriver side of the raft and disappeared.

Fear clutched my heart, and I gasped. *My bride, my love. Oh my God!* I stood up, left the oars and scrambled to the front of the boat to see her small, delicate right hand protruding from the water and grasping the safety rope that runs around the exterior of the raft tubes. I have always loved her beautiful hands. The rest of her was underwater and somehow she was being pulled back up river and under the raft. Todd had grabbed her arm and was holding on. Todd and I tried to pull her in. It is very hard to pull someone out of even slow-moving water over raft tubes twenty inches in diameter, much less out of a boiling, seething rapid. We managed to get her head and shoulders above water, and after struggling for a moment I grabbed the back of the waistband of her denim shorts and together, and with the help of an adrenalin boost, we hoisted her over the tubes and back into the raft.

In the meantime, the raft had slipped off the rock and started down the rapid backwards, and full of water nearly to the top of the tubes. Carol began furiously pumping the bail pump, and Todd was bailing water with his cap (our bail bucket had broken loose during the ordeal and went downriver). Carol's adrenaline was also pumping, and she worked the bail pump so hard it broke. I heard her scream one of the few cuss words I have ever heard come out of her mouth.

I battled to get the water-filled boat turned around and pointed downriver. It felt like it weighed a full ton and moved sluggishly and reluctantly. Just as I got pointed down the rapid, we hit a large rock head on and the force of the current, coupled with a boat heavy with water, caused the raft frame to shift forward and break one of the four tie down straps that secured the frame to the raft. The three remaining straps held, however, and we 'pin-balled' our way down the rest of the rapid, bouncing off every rock in that rapid.

Immediately below Blossom Bar Rapids lays Devil's Staircase

Rapids, where a long train of big standing waves run directly into a cliff face at an abrupt bend in the river. I knew we had to get to shore in the brief interlude of calm water just before Devil's Staircase. I again back ferried hard toward the right bank as Carol and Todd bailed water to lighten the load. We narrowly made it to a small beach, badly shaken but uninjured.

The rest of our party had stood by helplessly on the bank and watched in horror as the series of life-threatening predicaments befell us. They made their way along the cliffs and boulders of the right bank and joined us on the tiny beach where we had finally landed the raft. It was a joyful reunion, a look of relief evident on their faces.

Although it was just after noon, and still raining lightly, Dale decided we should make camp, start a fire and get Carol dried out and warm. He knew of a good site just below Devil's Staircase. We finished bailing out the raft, and had no trouble in the Staircase rapid, and landed on a nice beach called Gleason's Bar, where we set up our camp. Shivering in a blanket by the fire, Carol explained that she had felt our raft was hopelessly 'pinned' to the rock, and we would all have to get on the rock and wait for rescue.

Finally warm and dry and in the tent, Carol had nightmares that night, and for a year after. They were always the same. She relived the event but with one difference, she didn't make it back into the raft and bounced down through the rapid, crashing into rocks more underwater than above. Then she would wake.

The next morning we faced a half-day trip to the takeout at Foster Bar. There were only a couple of class II and III rapids that presented any concern. Carol had a rough night, and I knew she was apprehensive, but she boarded the raft without complaint, if a little tightlipped. We ran the rest of the river to the takeout without further incident. The weather even improved.

The following year we made the same Rogue River trip with some of the same friends. At the scouting site at Blossom Bar

Rapids I suggested to Carol she might want to walk around the rapid with Glenda (who continued to do so). I knew Carol was game, but it was *my* confidence that was a little shaky. She said she trusted me and preferred to go in the raft. *That's very courageous*, I thought. I needed her vote of confidence and she knew it. We ran Blossom Bar perfectly.

I have always admired Carol for her willingness to continue to raft rivers. She told me recently, "After our incident at Blossom Bar I knew you would always take care of and protect me."

Over the next twenty years, running rivers became the highlight of our summer vacations. Along with our group of river-loving friends we floated the Rogue many times, and also the Deschutes, Main Salmon, Lower Salmon and Middle Fork of the Salmon.

Ron and Carol negotiating Blossom Bar Rapids on the Rogue River

*Planning Team
at Old Chief
Joseph's grave,
Wallowa
County*

*Planning Team
at Hat Point,
HCNRA*

*Wedding of
Ron and Carol
in Baker City,
Oregon*

Dan, Todd, Carol, Ron and Trina

CHAPTER SIX

The Siskiyou National Forest

Wow! A forest supervisor! Attaining the position was a process akin to receiving knighthood. The chief of the U.S. Forest Service in Washington, D.C. had touched the sword to my shoulders.

It was a heady and sobering experience as the realization began to set in. I would be entrusted with the protection and management of over a million acres of public land, and the lives and careers of several hundred employees – a serious responsibility. I felt both grateful and humbled.

Carol was able to transfer from her regional office job to a position in personnel management on the Rogue River National Forest. She later moved to a position in their contracting department. The Rogue River Forest was headquartered in Medford, a city southeast of Grants Pass that was about an eighty-mile round-trip commute.

Warren Olney was the forest public information officer. He was the public face of the Siskiyou National Forest. He had a good sense of the major issues and controversies brewing in the local communities located around the forest. He also knew and was well known by media representatives, key people and service organizations. He had lined up a series of informal meetings, luncheons and evening socials and meetings with most of them so I could become acquainted in a short period of time with the local 'movers and shakers'.

So it was during my first few weeks of my assignment to the

Siskiyou National Forest that I met with the employees of the forest, the key players of the timber industry, environmentalists and local government officials. In a few hectic weeks I acquired a preliminary understanding of the land, the natural resources and related issues.

There was also the nagging feeling, sometimes a hazy image of dramatic social and cultural change on the horizon. It was headed our way, and I was learning that the implications would not be easily accepted by the good folks of Grants Pass, Cave Junction, Brookings, Gold Beach and Powers.

The time was well spent. A conceptual framework of what I wanted to accomplish long term and needed to do short term was taking shape in my mind.

Internally, I wanted to forge a highly functional management team of staff and rangers, improve our communication skills, and learn to share authority and responsibility. I wanted to increase the level of the direct participation of the forest specialists, the wildlife and fisheries biologists, landscape architect, archeologist, ecologist and botanist, in our decision-making process. When the going got tough, and I sensed that was our destiny, we would need our specialists, each with a long tenure and a reservoir of resource knowledge, on board with the forest management team. This included Lee Webb, Tom Atzet, and Don King. They had all earned outstanding credibility with our publics.

And I wanted to fan the flame of the indomitable spirit that I sensed smoldered on this forest.

Externally, I wanted to bring the environmentalists to the table. Move them from their refuge of alienation and confrontation they had created to a place of participation and constructive dialogue. I wanted to first personally acknowledge and then get acceptance of the fact that they were legitimate stakeholders and part of our public. I felt they had much to offer.

I wanted to bring the timber industry to the table with the

environmentalists. There were some good people in the industry, but they were having difficulty acknowledging, even to themselves, that public attitudes about logging were changing. I believed in the careful, scientific harvest of trees, and that our state and the nation would continue to need a viable wood products industry into the future. However, to get in step with the evolving public expression of what they wanted from their national forests I was confident we must:

1. Move away from clear-cutting as the principal timber harvest system on the Siskiyou.

2. Reduce the annual sale quantity to a more realistic level consistent with wildlife, fisheries and other ecosystem values.

I did not see this as an either/or issue. I fervently believed there were ways to have both a timber harvest program, clean water running through pristine river canyons, and wilderness. We just had to discover the way – together. I wanted to step back from warfare to negotiation.

I also wanted to enlist local political leaders, interested citizens and the forest management team in an ongoing issue resolution, and a resource management planning process that was inclusive and fully participative.

Finally, I planned to deliver a message to all of our publics. 'There is a new and creative way to do business and resolve issues on the Siskiyou National Forest. You are invited to get on board with us, and we will all move ahead together.'

A Bitter Legacy

In the early 1980s the Siskiyou Forest undertook an aggressive program to reduce vegetative competition to recently planted conifers in plantations within clear-cuts across the forest. This competition by brush species was a serious problem in getting the new young trees established. Application of herbicides was the most cost-effective method to reduce brush competition, applied mostly by helicopter, and sometimes manually by backpack sprayer.

The use of herbicides was very controversial. Especially in and around the small community of Takilma, whose origins were those of a counter-culture commune. In one unfortunate event of the recent past, a group of environmental activists physically prevented Forest Service workers from spraying a nearby plantation, going so far as to attempt to cut the backpack straps from the backs of workers. This very aggressive tactic frightened and angered the workers. Law enforcement was called in, and people were arrested. That unfortunate event and criminal act soured the employees of the Siskiyou Forest on environmental activists.

Early 1983, a few months before I arrived on the forest, a major new road was under construction in the heart of the forest. It was designed to access the stands of timber on the flanks of Bald Mountain and beyond.

Bald Mountain is a 3,811-foot-high prominence on a ridge that forms the northern boundary of the Kalmiopsis Wilderness. To the immediate north were 100,000 acres of roadless, undeveloped and very wild country. The wood products industry wanted the Forest Service to access that timber. Environmental groups desperately wanted to keep it roadless – a possible future addition to the existing Kalmiopsis Wilderness. One loosely organized but particularly aggressive group called themselves 'Earth First!'.

One night that summer, a group associated with Earth First! worked all night to block the road that was under construction. Their plan was to create enough of a barrier that it would take several hours to clear. Long enough to delay log truck drivers in their task to haul out right-of-way logs, and frustrate the Forest Service, the road contractor, and Josephine County sheriff's deputies. Long enough, perhaps, to get some good TV and newspaper coverage of the incident and gain regional or perhaps national attention.

The barrier consisted of chaining and padlocking protestors to the Forest Service steel gate that was closed each night following the road construction work. In addition, one activist had volunteered to lie in a trench and be buried up to his chin. It would take some time for the sheriff to dig him out, and it would make a great photo for the front page of the *Grants Pass Daily Courier*. The rest of the group carried signs declaring the travesty of constructing a road into this primitive area.

One of the activist protesters was a local environmentalist known as 'Bobcat'. Thin, even gaunt, with a long flowing beard and shoulder-length hair, he appeared as the quintessential latter-day flower child or hippie. He was reputed to have an advanced degree in physics. I was to learn that Bobcat was frequently behind the scenes as an organizer and strategist.

Early the next morning the first log truck topped the rise just before the gate. The driver was astounded to see a band of twenty or so disheveled-looking characters standing in front of the gate, some were holding cardboard signs that proclaimed 'Save the North Kalmiopsis'. A disembodied head seemed to be lying at the base of the gate!

The driver radioed his office. "Base, this is 31, we have a blockade on the road, right at the gate. Better notify the sheriff and the Forest Service. What do you want me to do?"

Another protester was Lou Gold, a small, wiry man with a full beard and a long mane of hair. He often carried a long staff and the effect was the image of a prophet. A carefully conceived image, I suspected. Lou is a former college professor who taught American government and urban politics at Oberlin College and the University of Illinois. He left his academic career in the mid-1970s and made his way to Takilma, Oregon, and became an environmental activist. Bald Mountain and the North Kalmiopsis roadless area were to become a major focus in his new life, and it thrust him into the limelight as an icon of the environmental movement.

The protestors staged seven blockades and tree-sitting events that summer, and forty protestors were eventually arrested and jailed by the Josephine County sheriff. Lou was one of them.

In addition to generating attention via creative onsite protests, Earth First! and the Oregon Natural Resources Council initiated a second front – legal action. They petitioned for a preliminary injunction to halt construction of the road, and on July 14, 1983, it was granted by a federal court.

Thus, environmental activists were successful in keeping the North Kalmiopsis roadless. Their plan was to maintain the option to add the area to the existing Kalmiopsis Wilderness. Although these protests happened the summer before I arrived on the Siskiyou Forest, more roadblocks, tree sitting in the woods, and demonstrations in front of the forest supervisor's office were yet to occur. It was clear these folks had developed a strategy and were very committed to their cause.

In the aftermath of the 'herbicide wars' and Bald Mountain confrontations, I had inherited a tense atmosphere laced with anger, distrust and bitterness on both sides. One newspaper called it the 'timber wars'.

But I had a plan.

Eight Dollar Mountain

A few weeks before leaving Portland for Grants Pass, I was visited by a member of Nature Conservancy, Melody Allen. Nature Conservancy is a nonprofit organization dedicated to acquiring private wildlands that are perceived to be threatened by development. They typically hold those lands until they can be purchased by a federal or state government land management agency. Over the years I had developed respect and admiration for the organization. It quietly and effectively goes about its work, avoiding the fanfare and the self-serving publicity that is the hallmark of some environmental groups.

148

Ms. Allen brought to my attention a situation at Eight Dollar Mountain, located within the Siskiyou National Forest near the small town of Cave Junction. This unusual, cone-shaped mountain rises to four thousand feet above the Illinois River. It is otherwise unremarkable except for a collection of unusual and rare plants sustained in places on its serpentine-formed rocky hillsides, and in marshy areas at its base.

In this sense it was a botanical treasure. The mountain's name came from the folk legend that an explorer or prospector wore out an eight-dollar pair of new boots circling the rock-strewn base of the mountain.

The mountain supported on its rocky slopes a stand of somewhat stunted pine and fir, marginal for timber production. In the past, several areas had been mined for nickel ore. The underlying geological structure – serpentine rock – and its chemical makeup accounted for the stunted tree growth, and rare plants, including the insectivorous 'pitcher plant' (darlingtonia californica) which traps, dissolves and absorbs any hapless insect that enters its flower.

An oversimplified summary of the situation is that miners wanted to extract the ore, timber interests wanted to harvest the trees, and the Nature Conservancy wanted to protect the rare plants and this unusual ecosystem that was Eight Dollar Mountain.

By most measures this was not an intense controversy. Positions of the key players were clear, but emotions were not high, and it was not a high-profile win/lose public issue. I reasoned this would be a good initial project to launch an alternative approach to issue resolution – a process called consensus seeking. I felt we had a good chance for success. And we needed a success before moving on to engage the emotionally charged North Kalmiopsis roadless issue.

I knew I needed some help with the consensus seeking process. I liked Bob Chadwick for the task. In the late 1970s Bob was forest supervisor on the Winema National Forest in southeast Oregon. He was pioneering the concept of consensus seeking in resolving national forest resource management issues and conflicts. He felt there was a better way than demonstrations, confrontations, appeals and lawsuits.

Bob was of medium build with a full beard and a smiling, optimistic approach to life. His energy seemed boundless. During his early years on the Winema Forest he worked closely with the Klamath Indian Tribe. It was from their reservation that the national forest had been carved. The tribe's way of settling differences and reaching decisions involved sitting in a circle, listening with respect, and slowly building agreement. Bob developed his approach to consensus seeking by learning the way of the Klamath Indian Tribe.

In our fast-paced and conflict-ridden world, his methods were unorthodox and controversial. He was the subject of ridicule among many of his contemporaries. I was intrigued by what he was doing, and I saw him as a brilliant pioneer in issue resolution techniques. His process was consistent with my beliefs on how people can work together. I asked Bob for his help on the Eight Dollar Mountain issue. I knew this would raise some eyebrows. I saw it as a way to announce that change had come to the Siskiyou! The first in a series of consensus meetings on Eight Dollar Mountain was set for March 1984.

Back at the supervisor's office I held my first meeting with the forest management team. I had some work to do at home before I waded too deeply into the resolution of major issues with our publics.

In the conference room I arranged the tables in the smallest square possible that would comfortably seat the five district rangers, eight staff officers and my secretary. Not quite a Klamath Indian circle in a teepee, but a move in that direction. I wanted to provide my team with some insight into my personal beliefs and management philosophy.

I began by saying, "I don't see myself as the brilliant leader who alone can provide all the answers and solve all our problems. However, I believe that I am good at establishing a climate for, and facilitating a team in issue resolution and decision making."

I paused and glanced around the room. I just saw nervous fidgeting and a few raised eyebrows. So I went on.

"I see myself as an open, informal person who prefers an organization that honors human values, yet works very hard. I believe in participative management. I am convinced that a group of people with common objectives can develop creative, realistic solutions. So, I will try to facilitate all of us in reaching a common understanding of what we want to do and where we want to go as a forest leadership team – and where we want to take this forest."

I paused again. This time there were a few nods of agreement.

"I say again, I will make a minimum of unilateral decisions. I intend to share leadership of this national forest with you. I realize this will be a change from what you have become accustomed to, and it just might frustrate some of you some of the time.

It will take time; I will ask you to work hard. At this point I need your patience and your support. I ask you to give this a chance. In order to sharpen our skills in this endeavor, we will likely engage in 'team-building' activities with an outside facilitator."

I asked if there were any questions or comments at this point.

A district ranger who had been shifting uneasily in his chair spoke up. "So far you have just talked about internal stuff, how about the land, the forest and its resources, what are your views on land management?"

"Good question," I said. "You deserve to know where I stand on this, probably the most important aspect of our mutual responsibility. I feel I have a very strong land ethic. I also believe we can construct roads and harvest timber on this national forest, but only accompanied by the highest standards of protection of the basic resources of watershed and water quality, wildlife and fisheries habitat, and soil productivity. I also believe wilderness is an important value of this forest. And so are old-growth forests. I want this forest to be on the leading edge of innovation in natural resource management."

I didn't get much response, and I didn't really expect much. I was the new guy, an unknown quantity and the boss. In their shoes I too would be very careful and reserved. I watched body language carefully. The reaction of the management team members seemed to range from guarded optimism through skepticism to disbelief. I knew I had a ways to go.

In retrospect, I had danced carefully around the subject of my 'land ethic'. In 1983 in southwest Oregon, and the Pacific Northwest in general, it was acceptable to talk openly about a land ethic in connection with resource extraction, but not environmentalism for its own sake. I had been influenced by early childhood hunting trips – many with my father – and my frequent long wanderings in Ober's Woods near my Ohio home. I had developed a kinship with the land and its creatures. Reading Leopold's *A Sand County Almanac* early in my career helped solidify these feelings into an operating philosophy about ecosystem health in connection with forest protection and management.

Some time before my retirement in 1990, Forest Engineer Dick Haines gave me a copy of his notes of that first meeting. Among other comments, he wrote, "It looks to me like what you said we were getting is what we got." That comment was important to me. I wanted to 'walk the talk'. I have always believed that being congruent is critical to achieving credibility.

It had become clear to me over the years that unilateral decision making didn't work well within most organizations, nor with the public (customers) it served. I had also learned that stakeholders in an issue resolution process must be party to the decision if they are to be committed to it. This was a simple management concept to espouse, but a difficult, time consuming, and often frustrating one to practice.

In the midst of being fully involved with my new job, helping Todd, Trina and Dan to get settled in their new schools, and Carol and I both juggling work schedules, I received a thick envelope in the mail from Jack Dinwiddie.

It was full of photos of the property he and his partner had recently purchased in Baja, Mexico. The photos were accompanied by a handwritten letter in Jack's characteristic scrawl, with an equally characteristic exclamation. "McCormick, this place is just frigging beautiful!" He described how he and his realtor friend, John Hensley, had purchased a parcel of land in the East Cape area of Southern Baja, Mexico (Baja Sur) along the Sea of Cortez. They were in the process of subdividing it and offering lots for sale to close friends. Their vision was to have a group of friends creating a rustic-style community in this isolated, harsh, but beautiful landscape.

Bruce and Judy Pewitt had already committed to purchase a lot.

I liked the Baja and was intrigued, but Carol and I had so much going on in our lives we decided we just couldn't focus on this opportunity. I returned the photos, thanked Jack and reluctantly declined, wistfully daydreaming about a winter vacation along a beach in the warm sun.

Building a Team

I scheduled a 'team-building' session with my new team of eight staff officers and five district rangers. The forest had been doing relatively well under the leadership of my predecessor. His management style had been effective but much more authoritative and directive than I would or could be. He made many unilateral decisions. I did not intend to operate in that manner, and I wanted to get through the 'mating dance' phases with my management team as quickly and effectively as possible.

I wanted relative isolation, no distractions, and privacy for this initial session. Someone, I believe it was Jerry Barrowcliff, the forest administrative officer, suggested an ideal location for our four-day session, a place called Steamboat Inn. It was an older resort on the banks of the North Umpqua River just east of Roseburg, a two-hour drive north of Grants Pass. It was pleasantly rustic, self-contained and relatively isolated. I also wanted an outside facilitator, but I felt that we were not ready yet for Bob Chadwick. Therefore, I contracted Northwest Executive Consultants, Inc. They were a more conventional choice, and I knew them to be very competent. The session was set for February 1-4, 1984.

Consultant Jerry Onken suggested that on the second morning of the session I be prepared to present a statement of my core beliefs, followed by my personal vision for the Siskiyou National Forest. I drafted it the evening we arrived, expanding the thoughts I expressed at our first management team meeting some time ago.

On that second morning I took a deep breath and presented them using an easel and chart paper. Here they are:

My Core Beliefs

1. I believe the work of the Forest Service to be of the highest value, and noble of spirit and intent. I feel that Forest Service employees deserve to feel good about the work they are involved in and proud to be part of the organization.
2. I believe that people basically want to do a good job, that we achieve fulfillment and self-esteem largely through our work.
3. I believe that the forest management team, with common goals and objectives, can together develop more workable solutions, make better decisions, and be more committed to them than if done independently or dependently. I believe that the

management team, together, can develop the 'vital few' (as opposed to the trivial many) issues we need to address, and fulfill the problem-solving, decision-making and program-development functions on this forest. I recognize that the forest supervisor must occasionally and unilaterally make the decision.

4. I prefer to manage and relate with emphasis on our shared humanism, letting our organizational positions play a secondary role in relationships.

5. I believe in operating in an open and cards-on-the-table manner. I don't see the necessity for, and do not like, agency secrets. I prefer to trust people (in and out of service) with information rather than to withhold or manipulate data.

6. I know that I, and most other people, need to be informed of 'how am I doing?' I believe people prefer to be held accountable for their work and thrive on positive feedback.

My Vision for the Forest

- The Siskiyou National Forest is a place – and fosters a climate – where employees feel good about their work and achieve growth, fulfillment, and satisfaction in their career and life.

- The Siskiyou develops and maintains a reputation as a forest that develops future leaders in the Forest Service. It becomes known as an exciting, progressive forest that nurtures its employees. On the leading edge of innovation, the Siskiyou is *the* place to be!

- The forest is known for attaining targets of goods and services with quality, efficiency and *style*.

- It's a can-do forest, willing to try innovative approaches to management.

- The public and cooperators respect the forest management team and employees as being an open, honest outfit; secure in its beliefs, firm and fair in its management.

I had taken about a half-hour to present this.

I finally paused, looked around the room and waited for a reaction. It was dead quiet. In this small room filled with five district rangers and eight staff officers no one said a word. Folks were staring at the chart paper and the vision statement. Disbelief? Suspicion? I didn't know.

No one wanted to be the first to respond. I finally asked Ted Stubblefield, the timber staff officer, what he thought. Ted had been acting forest supervisor between the time my predecessor left and I arrived. I had met Ted earlier (he was on the first Rogue River raft trip), and I liked and greatly respected him. So did the rest of the team members. I knew Ted's initial reaction could be influential.

Ted, built like a fire hydrant, square-jawed and with graying hair, was typically confident and self-assured. His opinion would carry a lot of weight. He leaned back in his chair and said, "I am just sitting here, letting it wash over me and enjoying it." Others nodded. I interpreted that as acceptance. I was grateful to Ted for supporting me at a critical time.

Reflecting on the day's events later that evening, I felt good and took encouragement in what I sensed was happening. There was a stirring, hopefully a reawakening of the collective spirit of the forest. The management team and the folks on the Siskiyou were beginning to believe that they could affect their destiny, that they could make a difference; and that they could become part of a team and forest recognized nationally as leaders in forest resource protection, management, and public involvement.

The Political Landscape

Up to this time, in order to be a successful politician in Southwest Oregon, one had to be supportive of resource extractive industries, particularly the timber industry.

Whether it be city councilor, county supervisor, congressman or senator, you were likely not going to get elected, and certainly not re-elected, if you did not clearly support the industry.

However, in 1984 Southwest Oregon was beginning to experience a shift in the way some publics viewed the national forests and their natural resources. In tandem with the urbanization of the west, the environmental movement was growing in both size and influence. I sensed we were on the cusp of a tide of significant change. The timber industry, local political leaders and vested interests were in denial.

I was sure that one way or another the volume of timber harvested from national forests in the northwest was going to be reduced. My strong belief was that in order for the Forest Service professionals, including foresters, biologists, hydrologists, ecologists and engineers, to have a hand in how this reduction was going to unfold, we needed to resolve local forest issues locally.

I believed the resolution of this larger issue would have to be with the participation and support of all the stakeholders – timber industry, environmentalists, interested residents, local leaders, politicians and the Forest Service as chief facilitator. Otherwise I believed it would be settled by the courts, or even more likely, politicians. If that happened, all of us locally would be left out of the process.

The Eight Dollar Consensus Process

The first consensus session regarding the fate of Eight Dollar Mountain was held in the spring of 1984, starting at midmorning in the conference room of the supervisor's office in Grants Pass. Representatives of the Forest Service, Bureau of Land Management, State of Oregon, Nature Conservancy and local citizens known to have an interest were invited. I was worried that some important notables might not show up. I always worried and fretted.

Bob Chadwick smiled patiently and said, "Trust the process, Ron, those that need to be here will be here." He rarely worried.

Before folks arrived, Bob asked me to help him move the

157

tables and arrange the chairs in a circle. We pushed all the tables to one side of the large room. As people drifted in they looked at this tight circle of chairs in the center of the room and their faces reflected puzzlement and a growing apprehension. Something different was going on here!

Bob smiled and beckoned them to sit down. They all found a seat, about twenty-five of us in all. I chose a chair across the circle from Bob. Initially, I, and most others I suspect, felt exposed and uncomfortable in this arrangement. Naked, as it were, shoulder to shoulder and with no table to hide behind, staring at one another across the circle.

Bob began by welcoming everyone in his smiling, relaxed manner. There was something about him that put people at ease. He exuded confidence, but his demeanor was friendly and non-threatening. At that point he knew none of the participants except me. He said he would like to start by conducting an exercise he termed 'grounding'. He asked each participant in turn around the circle to respond to a question: 'What did you give up to be here today?' Or 'How do you feel about being here today?'

The idea, I learned, was to help each person get their voice into the room from the very start, thereby establishing their right and ability to do so. It also caused them to get focused on the 'here and now' as he called it. To set aside the other aspects of their busy lives for the moment. Each person was given a minute or so to respond. He instructed everyone else to listen carefully and with respect.

In a way, sitting with others in a circle, my identity and mantle of forest supervisor became less important. I became one of them, a person with concerns and a keen interest in the welfare of Eight Dollar Mountain. The circle had a leveling effect. A lot of learning about each other happened in that half-hour of this first round. And amazingly, Bob had learned and remembered each person's name.

Following the introductory round, he posed a question and

asked each participant to respond, in turn. He asked, "What, from your point of view, would be the best outcome of these meetings?" And later a third round, "What are your worst fears about where this exercise might lead us?"

He would list each response on chart paper and post them around the room for all to see. At this point he would allow no responses or counter argument. This pattern was followed for the rest of the day.

Progressing around the circle provided each person an opportunity to speak, while Bob encouraged the rest to concentrate on listening. He eventually constructed lists of desired outcomes on one sheet, and concerns and worst fears on another. We could all see and understand these as comprising a graphic snapshot of the Eight Dollar Mountain issue.

We engaged in a series of consensus-building meetings throughout the summer. In time participants became more accustomed and comfortable with his approach. He started each meeting with a 'grounding' question, always different from the last meeting.

As we progressed, he often brought in experts on subjects such as minerals, timber resources and rare plants. We also took a field trip to Eight Dollar Mountain, led by an eminent professor of botany from Southern Oregon State University. This education helped the group slowly develop a common knowledge base, an understanding of the issues, and an appreciation for the resources and values of Eight Dollar Mountain. Most importantly, individuals began to discover common values and areas of agreement and disagreement. And mutual respect was growing.

Over the course of subsequent meetings we developed possible solutions and carefully built agreements on what needed to be done. The end result was a draft paper of management guidelines for Eight Dollar Mountain that all participants could support. We had consensus, or nearly so. It was certainly slow, hard work. I must admit I was growing impatient. However, the process eventually led the way to cooperative and successful protection and management of the area, and that was our goal.

But beyond that, this event announced and demonstrated to our publics a problem-solving and decision-making model and style that was fully participative and achieved agreement.

I liked the initial 'grounding' exercise and what it accomplished so much that I adopted it for most of my future staff and forest management team meetings. Going forward, I continued to use the consensus approach to resolve a series of management issues and conflicts. This included the Port-Orford-cedar root rot disease issue, wherein we received a notice in the form of a legal brief from the Oregon Natural Resources Council (ONRC) that they intended to take us to court over logging in the wet season and thereby spreading this waterborne disease.

Frankly, ONRC was correct in that we had placed this issue on the 'backburner'. I proposed that as an alternative to resolving this in court, they help us develop guidelines for curtailing the disease and protecting and managing this valuable tree. They eventually agreed, and we initiated a second participative and problem-solving group using the consensus process. I learned a lot from Bob Chadwick.

I was leading the forest staff in new and different directions and had a tendency to take on more than we could handle. Jerry Barrowcliff was in charge of personnel and the budget and was a member of the forest management team. I soon learned he was much more than just employees and numbers.

Jerry was thoughtful, quiet and reserved. Until he told me I would have never guessed he had been in the Army Airborne. He had been on the forest for several years, knew a lot of the recent history, and had good judgment. He would come into my office at times and ask to sit down for a quiet talk. I always obliged because I learned he had observed something or sensed something I needed to know. He would show up when he thought I was veering off course, taking on too much, or about to unknowingly commit a fiscal irregularity. I appreciated his quiet, measured counsel, and trusted his advice.

Confrontation – The Timber Industry

In the early 1980s, the wood products industry, commonly called the timber industry, was big business in Southwest Oregon, comprised of the counties of Coos, Douglas, Jackson and Josephine. Large sawmills and plywood mills owned and operated by nationally known companies were the industrial engines of commerce in these four counties. Economies of local communities revolved around the harvest and milling of lumber and the production of plywood and other wood products from the old-growth Douglas-fir, ponderosa pine, Port-Orford-cedar and other local species.

Federal lands are exempt from county or state taxes. Per the twenty-five percent fund act of 1908, and to offset this lack of tax revenue, the counties received twenty-five percent of the annual gross timber sale receipts from timber sales from national forest lands within the individual counties. These funds, by federal law, were earmarked to be used for schools and roads. To varying degrees the counties had become dependent on these receipts. All residents benefited as the timber sale receipts offset individual property taxes. Thus property taxes had historically been low in these counties. The industry, local politicians and most citizens understandably wanted to maintain the status quo.

My first major meeting with all of the Southwest Oregon timber industry officials came on December 4, 1984 at Herbs La Casita Restaurant in Grants Pass. I had previously met with individual mill owners and industry representatives, and those encounters had all been cordial. This was my first formal meeting with all of them as a group. All of the local sawmill and plywood mill owners or managers from the communities of Grants Pass, Cave Junction, Medford, Brookings, Gold Beach and Roseburg were present.

Also prominently in attendance were the representatives of The Southern Oregon Timber Industry Association (SOTIA), Douglas Timber Operators (DTO) from Roseburg, and the Northwest Timber Association representatives, who came down from Portland. These were paid representatives of the several large timber industry associations. We in the Forest Service called them 'hired guns'. They were professional and good at what they did. I think they liked the gunfighter image.

I had already put together the Eight Dollar Mountain consensus group and had held the first of a series of meetings to develop the Land and Resource Management Plan for the Siskiyou National Forest (the Forest Plan). These public involvement meetings were designed to divide the large audience into smaller groups that represented a mix of interests – timber industry, local government representatives, environmentalists and members of the general public. Each group was led by one of a cadre of skilled group facilitators I had borrowed from other national forests.

I knew going in that the industry, and particularly the industry representatives, did not like this approach to resolving the inevitable conflicts between logging and other forest values. They did not want participative planning (consensus seeking) to become the format for forest planning on the Siskiyou, fearing it might spread to the rest of Oregon.

I understood that, and in a way I couldn't fault them. The timber industry had been very successful in maintaining Annual Sale Quantities (ASQ) from national forests in the Pacific Northwest via establishing and maintaining close working relationships with key Forest Service personnel. They liked to consider us 'partners' in a common cause, and they wanted us to feel that way also. Frankly, I did not see it that way. I had always felt I represented all of the public, and all the forest resources, in protecting and managing the publicly owned lands we called the national forests.

The industry employed full-time representatives to influence forest supervisors and local congressional staffers, and exert political pressure in Washington, D.C. The industry represented significant campaign contributions. Sitting down with other publics, with diverse and often contrary interests, to resolve differences did not fit well with the established process and only spelled loss. I knew I was going against the grain.

I was not deterred. I had decided to use this meeting to explain my approach to forest planning and issue resolution – namely bringing all the 'stakeholders' to the table and work together for decisions and solutions that all could support.

They were 'laying' for me.

I had made only the introduction of my short presentation when they began, one after the other, to hammer on me about participative planning and particularly 'Consensus' with a capital C. The word was anathema to them.

"Why are you catering to these 'eco freaks', don't you realize they are our mutual enemy?" the lead representative asked. Before I could reply a second representative chimed in.

"Why would you collaborate with our enemy?"

Then a third added, "These 'long hairs' do not deserve a place at the table, this is crazy, we will not support this approach."

Their attacks quickly became personal, and in turn they continued to toss caustic comments and questions at me. They called me naïve and out of step.

I recognized there was another dynamic at work here. They were playing to their employers, the mill owners, who were also present. The representatives were intent on demonstrating how they could beat up the new forest supervisor; and in so doing, highlighting the importance of their role in the timber wars to come.

When I was finally afforded an opportunity to speak, I patiently tried to explain the requirements of the National Environmental Policy Act (NEPA) and the National Forest Management Act (NFMA) that both required public participation. After an hour of having my concepts challenged and belittled, my composure was on the wane, so I concluded my presentation and sat down before my anger and frustration overcame my better judgment. Soon thereafter the meeting was mercifully adjourned.

My staff and district rangers who were present were embarrassed for me and upset with the industry representatives. I had taken a beating, and everyone knew it. I was shaken, and I knew I could not let this stand.

A few days later I called the same industry representatives and set up a private meeting with them on neutral turf in Eugene, a small city about a two-hour drive north of Grants Pass. No audience, no mill owners. I didn't explain. I just said I wanted them there. They showed up, not knowing exactly what to expect, but not confident enough to ignore the new supervisor of an important forest with substantial timber resources. I was counting on that.

I took one of my staff officers along, Bob Ettner, who was in charge of forest planning. I did this partly to have a witness, and partly so word would get back to the rest of the folks on the forest that I was not going to 'roll over' for the timber industry 'hired guns'.

It was a short meeting. There was no audience to play to, and it was my turn.

"I will not be treated in the manner of the recent meeting," I said. "I have no trouble with disagreement. But if you folks want a working relationship with me, and I think you do, I insist it be one of mutual respect."

"Oh, Ron, you took the last meeting too seriously and personally," one retorted. "We think you misunderstood our intentions."

"I understood your intentions very well. I will have none of it in the future," I concluded.

We then engaged in twenty minutes of cordial 'small talk' about specific timber sales, the price of logs, etc. From that time forward our meetings, though tense, were without the personal jibes and cheap shots that characterized the initial confrontation.

The Nature of the Siskiyou National Forest

I have described the cultural and political climate of the times in some detail, but I have not described the forest itself. It is time to remedy that.

The Siskiyou is a 1.1-million-acre national forest in southwest Oregon occupying the mountainous terrain between the little community of Powers to the north, the California /Oregon border to the south, Grants Pass to the east and Gold Beach to the west. It is transected by the Rogue, Illinois and Chetco Rivers that run from the mountains to the sea.

The name 'Siskiyou' means 'bobtailed horse' in the Chinook-Cree Indian language, and apparently it is in reference to a horse lost in the area during one of the first fur expeditions in the early 1800s.

At first glance the forest's jumbled array of ridges and streams does not present an awe-inspiring landscape as compared to the snow-capped Cascade or Sierra Nevada ranges. This forest is not about grandeur. However, a closer inspection reveals a rich, unusual diversity of plants, wildlife and fish. The unique values of the Siskiyou Forest are often at one's feet.

A Forest Service brochure states:

> *The Siskiyou area embodies the most complex soils,*
> *geology, landscape, and plant communities in the Pacific*
> *Northwest. World-class wild rivers, biological diversity,*

> *remarkable fisheries resources, and complex watersheds*
> *define the Siskiyou. It is the most floristically diverse*
> *national forest in the country....*

This national forest also offers significant economic value, including expansive Douglas-fir and ponderosa pine forests, and mineralized areas offering gold and chromium. There was a history of logging and mining, with local communities depending on these resources to supply sawmills, plywood mills and mineral extraction industries. It had become tradition, and the economic mainstay of Josephine and Curry Counties. Economists had coined a term for these situations that had become common across the Western United States – 'timber dependent communities'.

However, changing values and an evolving urban culture forecast a transition to a different economy, and therein lay the seeds of conflict and turmoil.

A lot was made of the subject of individual 'management styles' in the late 1960s and 1970s. Some great leaders such as Winston Churchill, Teddy Roosevelt and Margaret Thatcher epitomize the capacity and ability to make bold individual decisions. Others, such as President Jimmy Carter, preferred a consensus style. History seems to laud the former. Although I admired people with this ability, I new it wouldn't work for me. Early on, as I worked my way up the ladder to positions with increasing management and supervisory responsibility, I intuitively gravitated to more of a consensus-seeking leadership style. It just felt better. The U.S. Forest Service was and is a line and staff type organization, not unlike the military. Staff officers provided the information, and line officers made the decisions. Any other style made some people uncomfortable, but I intended to blur the boundary between the line and staff functions.

It was also time to send a message to the public describing how I intended to operate. I intended for my internal management style to be consistent with our interactions with our publics. Our public, or customers if you will, were the timber industry, environmentalists, community and county government, and the media.

My pursuit of building a new forest management team internal operating style, and a renewed forest attitude and spirit, was coming to fruition. Going forward I knew we would need to be at our best. I had an inkling of what was coming, but I did not fully envision or comprehend the magnitude of what was about to unfold: The disastrous fires of 1987, the spotted owl controversy, proposals to bring to a halt all timber harvest and convert the national forest to a national park, a wood products industry intent on maintaining high harvest levels, and heavy-handed political intervention.

Social Change

The brochure I described earlier should have mentioned that the Siskiyou Forest was also home to one of the most diverse publics in the Pacific Northwest, with the extremes of ultra-conservative right wingers and anti-government 'survivalists' to middle-of-the-road pro-business types to commune-dwelling environmental purists. And all were amply represented.

Folks with a different view of society, and particularly public land management, had found their way to rural Southern Oregon in the 1960s and established themselves near the rural towns of Cave Junction and Williams. Sometimes they were referred to as the 'counter-culture', or, if you didn't like what they stood for, 'hippies'. These were mostly very bright and always very committed people who had been vocal and active over the years advocating their preference for preservation over active management as a public land management precept. They opposed commercial forestry, the use of herbicides, road building and in particular 'clear-cutting' of trees. Add to this the evolving societal view of public land values.

I had been aware since my California assignments and Don

Bauer's coaching that as the West developed and evolved into an urban society, so did the urban citizens' view of the national forests change and evolve. The natural resource extraction and use mindset of the residents of the rural, small towns was beginning to be overshadowed by the more preservation-minded residents of cities and suburbs. As with many social changes, this happened first in California. And with the in-migration to Oregon of escapees from the large cities of California, new ideas were arriving in Southern Oregon. This reached an inflection point in the 1987 to 1990 period. The course for dramatic change in public land stewardship was set.

Externally, we were forging a stronger participative relationship with our publics through consensus seeking and full participative decision making. We were developing the first forest plan to be completed in Western Oregon via an unprecedented level of public involvement and hands-on participation, but always amid entrenched positions and sometimes the outright opposition of special interest groups. Then we were waylaid by the monstrous Silver and Longwood Fires of that most terrible fire year, 1987. And finally the fire recovery and timber salvage effort, which more than anything else, brought to a head the rancor and bitterness between the timber industry and the environmental organizations.

During this time the level of political involvement at the local, state and federal level grew to the point where we were experiencing not only a high level of interest, but direct intervention.

The Forest Plan

The National Forest Management Act (NFMA) was signed into law in 1976. The act mandated sweeping changes as to how the nation's public forests were to be managed, requiring Forest Land and Resource Management Plans to be developed for each national forest with public involvement, and a draft then a Final

Environmental Impact Statement. There had been delays getting started on the planning due to disagreements and infighting among interest groups at the national level – primarily the timber industry and environmental organizations – as to what the act meant and required.

At the time I arrived on the forest in late 1983, the forest planning staff and resource specialists had made several attempts to turn out a draft plan, but for reasons internal, external and political, they had never been able to publish a draft plan and DEIS. I spoke with each person involved. It became clear to me that a series of false starts over several years, characterized by uncertainty and changes in requirements, had left this group discouraged, demoralized and fast approaching burnout. The planning staff officer was eligible, and wanted, to retire. I was worried about the planning folk's morale, and their ability to muster the energy and enthusiasm to take a new approach to producing a plan.

We really had to have our act together for this final, coordinated push. It was going to be controversial and of high profile. So I enlisted the help of Bob Chadwick one more time to facilitate and lead us in a team-building exercise.

I made arrangements to meet for three days at a facility away from the office and family, and I asked – required is more accurate – the management team to attend. This time I also included the forest specialists: wildlife biologist, fisheries biologist, archeologist and landscape architect. We were functioning pretty well by now, but I wanted to integrate the specialists as part of the team and put a final polish on our interrelationships. It went well. We came out of that session as a tight, committed group of people. I felt we were finally a team. We were going to get it done!

We were determined to produce a sound, realistic and balanced plan that reflected all of the resources and distinctive values of the Siskiyou – of which timber was only one.

We also wanted a high degree of citizen and interest group

involvement in the process, and as much 'hands-on' as we could manage. I let the team know I wanted the Siskiyou Forest to have the first draft plan published in the Pacific Northwest. Jaws dropped, but the folks accepted the challenge. Why not? We were the best!

Instead of just a public meeting, the forest planning group, on their own initiative, designed an initial round of participative work sessions with the public set for November 17, 1984. Entering the large conference room of the Riverside Motel, the site of the first work session, environmentalists along with wood products industry people were filing in. I encountered Russ McKinley, forester for the large Boise Cascade Corporation's sawmill operation in Medford. I liked Russ, and thought him a reasonable person, but in a tight lipped fashion he told me, "We warned you not to do something like this, but you did it anyway." He turned away obviously upset. I also saw Ann Basker, a County Commissioner for Josephine County. She proffered a wry smile and said, "God, I hate NEPA."

In the meantime Lou Gold had taken up residence on Bald Mountain in the heart of the controversial roadless area on the edge of the Kalmiopsis Wilderness. He garnered some publicity for his cause in doing so, which irked some locals and a few of my staff. I liked to get out in the field with the management team, and thought it would be both instructive and fun to hike into Lou's camp and stay overnight in the forest. I thought of it as a field oriented 'team building.' There was some grumbling and a little apprehension, and a few thought we should forcefully eject Lou from his camp rather than pay him a friendly visit. Lou had learned we were coming, and had prepared a walking stick replete with carved inscriptions and colorful ribbons for each of us. They were made from the dead lower limbs of a large old-growth Douglas fir that grew near his camp. I still have mine.

Foot in Mouth Disease

In June 1987, the *Grants Pass Daily Courier* wanted to conduct an interview on the final version of the new Forest Plan we were developing. They assigned their lead reporter, Paul Fattig, to do the story. I suggested to Paul that we take a field trip through the forest to look at current forest management practices and talk about the upcoming plan. Paul and the *Courier's* photographer, Tim Bullard, and I spent a morning touring the forest, looking at cutting units, reforestation projects, streamside protection practices, and fisheries habitat improvement projects. I wanted to avoid specifics as our draft Forest Plan had not yet been reviewed and cleared by the regional forester and chief's office. Up to that point I felt the tour was going very well.

On the drive back to town Paul was sitting in the back seat when he leaned forward and asked me a leading question. It was a question I had been anticipating, even aching to answer, but I knew danger lurked in my answer. I believe Paul sensed this, and being a good reporter he asked it: "What do you think the annual timber harvest volume should be in the future?"

I was driving, and I had to twist around in my seat to answer. I felt it important I catch his eye, and over my shoulder I answered.

"I would have some trouble if we had to sustain the nearly 200 million board-foot annual timber sale level going forward."

I just blurted it out. I had always found it hard to suppress what I knew to be the truth. I also knew there would be consequences, even though my statement reflected the current science and the best judgment of my district rangers, planning staff and myself.

On June 9, a well written, positive article entitled '*Forest Supervisor stands between land, people*' appeared in the *Courier*. It detailed the positive land management practices the forest was currently implementing, and importantly, I thought, described our hands-on public participative approach to forest planning, consensus building, and conflict resolution. It was placed in the middle of the paper in the Community section.

However, it was the headline. The front page shouted, *'Supervisor says Forest Service must slow down'*. As I read it I thought, *Oh shit! This will be trouble.*

A few days later a phalanx of sawmill owners, SOTIA representatives and a few others demanded an immediate audience, which I granted. They expressed their extreme displeasure about the headline and article and demanded I retract my statements about reducing the forest's annual timber sale quantity. I politely declined, saying we had been cutting too much for several years on the forest, and in the interest of sustainable forest management, a reduction in the cut was the right thing to do. They left in a huff, dissatisfied and angry.

The following week a previously scheduled two-day meeting for the Pacific Northwest Regional Leadership Team was held in Eugene. This was one of about four such meetings held annually, and they were a big deal. The regional forester, his three deputies, and all twenty regional staff directors were present, as well as the forest supervisors of each of the nineteen national forests in Oregon and Washington. It was a large group, and the meeting was held in a main ballroom of the Hilton Hotel. Forest planning was the first and principle topic.

The regional forester stood at his podium and opened the meeting, saying he had just concluded a phone conversation with Chief Robertson in Washington, D.C. He paused, ominously, I thought, and then went on.

"The chief said he cannot stand any more statements from the forests of the Pacific Northwest Region that the ASQ (annual sale quantity) should or would be reduced."

The regional forester asked two forest supervisors to stand up - me and one other supervisor from another forest. I squirmed in my seat a bit, and then rose to my feet. The rest of the group stared. Following an uncomfortable pause, the regional forester resumed his lecture.

"I do not want to see or hear about any more stories in newspapers or TV news about reducing the cut." He paused for effect, and then added, "The chief just cannot stand the political heat at this time." He looked at me as he spoke, and with emphasis exclaimed, "And that means you, McCormick!"

I was embarrassed and hurt. I had offered the truth to the press, and the regional forester, and most everyone attending the meeting, knew it. What had transpired of course is that timber industry representatives had called one or more Oregon congressmen or senators, probably both, who in turn called the Assistant Secretary of Agriculture, who called the chief, who then called the regional forester, who had chosen to rebuke two of his forest supervisors publicly in the forum of this regional meeting. As a Marine Corps drill instructor told our platoon of wide-eyed recruits at the Parris Island boot camp many, many years earlier, "Shit runs downhill, and you skinheads are at the bottom of the hill!"

I had been stung once again by the 'timber imperative'. The first time in 1961 at Mad River on the Six Rivers Forest in California, the second on the Lolo National Forest in Missoula, Montana. And now in Oregon, I was disappointed, but by now not surprised.

Supervisor says Forest Service must slow down

By Paul Fattig
of the Daily Courier

The Siskiyou National Forest cannot continue producing its current timber harvest level if it is to provide a sustainable yield.

That was the candid conclusion drawn by forest Supervisor Ron McCormick during a recent tour of the forest.

"I would have some trouble if we had to sustain the 200-million-board-foot level for very many more years," McCormick said. "That could begin to have a detrimental effect on balanced management. I don't think we can sustain that level."

During each of the past two years, the forest has sold 200 million board feet of timber, McCormick said. Last year, about 190 million

■ Forest supervisor tries to be evenhanded.
Page 1C.

board feet was harvested, he added, noting that figure will be repeated this year.

About 470 million board feet of timber is currently under contract.

On a 10-year average, the current timber management policy calls for cutting about 167 million board feet each year to maintain a sustainable balance between harvesting and replanting, he said.

"For the past couple of years, we've been selling over what would be our average sell level," he said.

Although McCormick said the harvest level will be a tad below its average annual cut, he would not divulge the precise annual harvest recommended in the long-awaited draft 10-year forest plan. Although it has been held up by legal appeals and bureaucratic tangles, he expects the plan, which will be updated every decade, to be released in August.

"That would give us something to talk to," he said. "We've had to somehow defend a phantom forest plan that nobody has really seen. We want to get it out and explain the preferred alternative to the various user groups."

But he stressed the first plan is simply a draft, one which is expected to be revised.

"We're open to changes — we really mean that," he said. "It will be our first crack at what will be a pretty good balance for this forest.

"It's my intent that the final plan be a well-balanced plan," he said. "Part of our job with the plan is to help people define what they want their forest to be. We can interject our professional and scientific knowledge into that mix, but I don't think we alone can

Turn to TIMBER, Page 2A

Timber
Continued from Page One

dictate what it should be nor can any one interest group."

The point, McCormick stressed, is that both the timber industry and environmental communities should expect to compromise in the forest of the future.

For instance, 50 years from now, there will be fewer acres of old-growth timber, he said. By his count, there are about 400,000 acres of old-growth timber in the 1.1 million-acre forest.

"No matter what we do in planning, there will be more than 330,000 acres remaining," he said. "Part of that is in wilderness, part in botanical areas, in riparian areas."

However, the final acreage will depend on what alternative is selected in the forest plan, he said.

Moreover, roads will undoubtedly be punched into a large portion of areas that are now roadless, he said, estimating there are now about 300,000 acres of roadless areas outside wilderness sections.

"A large part of this forest's future harvest, while these replanted sites are growing, needs to

come out of roadless areas," he explained. "We'll have more roads than we do now, but we'll still have a viable forest ecosystem. I believe we'll maintain the diversity it has now."

McCormick is adamantly opposed to a proposal to create a 700,000-acre national park in the forest, noting that action would halve the forest's annual timber sale.

"That would have a dramatic effect on the local woods product industry and the local economy," he said. "There is no question about that."

The supervisor doesn't deny that the timber industry, like the environmental groups, applies pressure to the Forest Service.

"The industry has been quite successful at the national level in convincing Congress to keep sale targets for this region quite high," he said, noting that corresponded to an economic recovery in recent years.

The agency also is influenced by political appointees made by each administration occupying the

White House, he said.

"We have become somewhat more politicized in the last few years than we have been before," he said. "Every new administration comes in and makes a run to get control of the agency. We haven't abandoned our own precepts, but we have, and properly so, been more responsive to the administration currently in power."

Yet the agency also takes advantage of breakthroughs made in forest science, he said, citing slash burning as an example.

"The researchers are saying it's not a good idea to burn so clean like we have been doing," he said. "The fuels rot on the forest floor and all the critters use it. Both the bugs and the pathogens have a function. When we burn those and take it all out, it sets back the productivity."

As a result, foresters are beginning to leave more fuels to feed the growing forest, he said.

"We're finding that if we stay as close to the natural processes as possible, we're a heck of a lot better off," McCormick said.

A protest by Earth First! in front of the Supervisor's Office

Visiting Lou Gold on Bald Mtn. – before the fire

Siskiyou Forest Management Team

Cross Country skiing near Mt. Bachelor, Oregon

River running companions in camp on the Rogue River

CHAPTER SEVEN

The Silver Dragon

In the late summer of 1987 we were on schedule in developing the Forest Land and Resource Management Plan (Forest Plan) and the accompanying Draft Environmental Impact Statement (DEIS).

The process had been tedious and fraught with problems and delays, but we had forged ahead with determination. In mid-August of 1987 we published the Forest Plan and DEIS. After years of struggle, disappointments and setbacks, our forest planning team had persevered. We were all deservedly proud.

In order to recognize this milestone and the significance of the accomplishment, Carol and I hosted a celebration party and potluck in our backyard. We invited the entire management team, biologists and planning specialists. It was the evening of August 25, 1987.

Carol arranged for a cake decorated with a depiction of a stork holding the Forest Plan and DEIS in a bag in its beak. The bold inscription read: "Congratulations! Our new baby, 13 pounds, 14 ounces." This was the combined weight of the two large volumes of the Forest Plan and the DEIS. We were all feeling very good about the accomplishment, and looking forward to producing the final plan and EIS following the required public comment period.

Everything was going well, so Carol and I decided to treat ourselves to a few days off. One of our rafting friends had drawn a permit to float the wild section of the Rogue River and invited us to join the group. We were always up for a float trip!

Five days after the celebration party, we launched our rafts from the Argo boat landing just above the wild section of the river. It was Sunday morning, August 30, and we were on the river again with our longtime rafting companions Ted and Mary, and John and Glenda. We had been rafting together for several years by then and owned our own rafts and gear. We were all very competent on the river.

Summer came early in 1987 and remained hot and dry into August. The forecast was for continued hot and dry, with the promise of a hundred-degree afternoon and a slight chance of thunderstorms on the day we launched. The river was low, exposing more beaches for camping. We looked forward to a great trip.

In late afternoon, huge and threatening dark cumulus clouds began to build, and by early evening we heard distant thunder to the south.

We camped on a beach by the river's edge. We sat on lawn chairs with our bare feet in the cool water, which offered some relief from the oppressive heat. With a beer in hand and listening to the thunder in the distance, I reflected on some facts about wildfire that our forest ecologist, Tom Atzet, had related to me sometime earlier. He had said:

"Our research of the fire history suggests that the Siskiyou has a fire cycle, or periodicity, of about fifteen years." The ecologist went on. "This means that on average, over the past hundred years or so, major fires had sweep over the forest about every fifteen years. And we are long overdue for a big fire."

During the night, lightning flashed to the south of us almost continuously for over an hour, lighting up the narrow canyon. As the storm moved closer, the flashes were followed almost immediately by thunder reverberating off the canyon walls. It was nature's light and sound show! By morning the storm had passed, but there had been no rain. A dreaded 'dry' lightning storm!

The next day we traveled down river to the next campsite,

blissfully unaware of the large number of fires that had been ignited to our south, and were growing rapidly. The following morning I awoke at first light and peeked out of our tent. Drift smoke hung in the canyon, and its acrid smell stung my nose. I was suddenly very concerned. We all arose, and following a quick breakfast, launched our boats and pushed downriver to the historic Rogue River Ranch, situated on a bench just above the river and along Mule Creek. The Bureau of Land Management (BLM) had a volunteer caretaker stationed there, and I knew he had radio contact with the nearest lookout tower. He was not around but had left a note tacked to the door. It read, 'Ron McCormick, urgent message, contact your office.' I thought, *Oh no, please not now.*

The forest's fire staff officer, Wayne Spencer, had anticipated I would stop at the ranch and had left me the message. I went inside and used the BLM radio and, via relay through a lookout tower, I reached my office. The fire dispatcher said, "Ron, we have multiple large fires, and I suggest you return home as soon as possible."

He wanted to send a helicopter for me, but we were above the class IV Blossom Bar Rapids and Carol did not want to try to row our raft and gear through it alone. Besides, I thought, Fire Staff Officer Wayne Spencer was an experienced and knowledgeable professional. He knew more about wildfire than I would ever know, and I had high confidence in his ability and judgment. I rationalized that a few hours delay on my part was not going to make a great deal of difference.

We had left our vehicles and raft trailers where we launched our rafts two days previous. They were to be shuttled later in the week to the Foster Bar boat landing. But now we were going to arrive at that take-out two days earlier than we had arranged with the shuttle service. I asked the dispatcher to contact the shuttle service at the Galice Store to have our vehicles and boat trailers shuttled to the Foster Bar take-out as soon as possible, no later than early afternoon.

We all rowed hard to push our rafts downriver, not even taking the time to scout Blossom Bar Rapids. We shouted to a group of folks at the scouting point on the rocks above to determine if the passage through this dangerous rapid was clear. It was, and one after the other we shot through and down the rapid without incident.

By now the canyon was choked with smoke, and it was a very unpleasant place to be. The rest of the party had decided they also wanted to leave. A few hours later we arrived at Foster Bar. As we approached I was relieved to see our vehicles and raft trailers in the parking area.

We loaded the raft on the trailer in record time, and Carol and I headed over Bear Camp Road, which crossed the mountains and was the shortest route to Grants Pass. The rest of the party decided to drive in the opposite direction to Highway 101, then home. I anticipated we might encounter one of the fires on our way over the pass.

We wound our way up the twisty grade, and it seemed to take forever. We encountered no traffic coming down. We worried that the road might have been closed ahead due to a fire. I pulled over at a viewpoint at Bear Camp summit, where we could see columns of dense smoke boiling out of at least two different locations on the forest. There was no sign of helicopters or retardant bombers.

"This is really serious," I told Carol. The fires were obviously large and growing. "I don't understand why there are no retardant bombers working the fires, or fire crews on this road." In fact, there was *no* one else on the road.

I had acquired a significant amount of wildland firefighting experience over my career, especially in California, and fully expected that by now there would be a flurry of fire suppression activity underway.

We crossed the summit and headed down toward Galice. We rounded a turn and suddenly there was fire on each side of the road. It was hot, the air filled with smoke and falling ash. Dodging burning logs that had rolled into the roadway, we made our way down to the junction of the Merlin-Galice Road, the still inflated raft on the trailer behind. I recall hoping burning embers would not fall into the raft and burn holes in it, but I didn't stop to check. There were no vehicles on the road, nor firefighters on the fire. *Where is everyone?* I recall thinking, over and over. I just could not understand it. Later, I was to learn that this was the Galice Fire, unattended at the time we dashed through it.

Our home was on the way to my office, so I took Carol there, where I unhitched the trailer and raft. I hurried to the office. I was not to see much of Carol for the next sixty days.

I was quickly briefed, and learned that a huge, dry lightning storm had moved up from Northern California, igniting fires all along the way. The Klamath Forest in Northern California had several large fires, as did the Siskiyou Forest. As the storm proceeded to our north, it remained active and started even more fires. The situation was quickly developing into a two-state disaster. The three largest fires on the Siskiyou had been named Galice, Longwood and Silver.

I asked Wayne why there were no fire retardant bombers, pumper trucks or crews working the fires Carol and I had observed on our way to Grants Pass. Wayne informed me, with frustration evident in his voice, that most of the region's available fire suppression resources, including those of the Siskiyou, had already been dispatched and committed to the earlier fires to the south that threatened the communities and residents of Happy Camp, Takilma and Cave Junction.

The fires on the northern half of the Siskiyou did not threaten homes and people, so we were at the bottom of the priority list for the limited amount of fire suppression equipment and fire crews available. I understood the explanation, but I didn't feel any better about the situation. This was my 'watch' over the Siskiyou, and I

181

harbored a deep sense of responsibility to protect this forest and its resources. However, for the time being we were on our own, with only a bare minimum of crews and equipment.

I learned that the Silver Fire had been reported at 10:30 p.m. on August 30, 1987. It was located in the isolated and extremely steep and rugged Silver Creek Canyon. I then realized I had at that very time been sitting on a small beach along the Rogue River, watching and listening to the approaching storm. At four a.m. the following morning the Lake of the Woods lookout reported that she could see a real good column of smoke in the Silver Creek area.

Smokejumpers!

The regional office had been in the process of repositioning crews and equipment to the south and had routed a plane filled with smokejumpers to Cave Junction. The forest had radioed the aircraft and had it redirected to the fire. Twenty-one brave people from Montana and Washington jumped into the dragon's mouth about eleven a.m. One jumper was injured. The fire activity continued to pick up, and the fire had grown to a hundred acres. The smokejumper squad leader had called in and reported a second fire just to their north, and in his opinion the two fires were going to soon merge. Air support from retardant tankers was not available. At about six p.m. the decision was made to evacuate the twenty-one jumpers before they became trapped and hurt. They were instructed to walk out.

In one official account the injured smokejumper, Leslie Anderson, sat on a ridge top nursing a badly sprained ankle and watched the fire approach. The report states:

> *She wondered how she would get out of there now that the requested helicopter was not coming. Leslie sensed that the fire was going to blow up. As it swept closer, Leslie describes its action as if the fire had a mind*

of its own. Due to the intense radiant heat, trees were rapidly igniting. They became super-heated and were instantly engulfed in flame from base to top. Giant trees going up in flame, one step at a time, left the image of an advancing fire-monster whose footsteps were consuming everything in its path.

The crew, now on foot and with a punishing effort, made their way across steep, brushy terrain and assisted Leslie to the nearest road, and safety, a few miles away.

The Klamath National Forest to our south also had several large fires; one threatened the community of Happy Camp. Our Longwood Fire threatened the communities of Takilma and Cave Junction. The Galice and Silver Fires that we had driven through on our way home from the river were a long way from towns and homes.

All available firefighting resources in the state had previously been committed to those fires on the Klamath Forest, and the Longwood Fire on the south end of the Siskiyou. Savings lives and property was the region's priority. No one was fighting the Silver Fire. We were down to a 'skeleton crew' on the forest, and on our own for the foreseeable future.

Fire crews finally began trickling in by September 4, and eventually a few fire pumpers, tractors and other equipment showed up. And the regional office was able to cobble together an incident command team with Dick Hodge from Idaho as incident commander (IC). I say cobbled together because all the organized teams were already committed.

In the meantime, the fire continued to grow. It made major 'runs' on September 3, and by early evening on September 4 had reached 18,000 acres. But we were still tagged with the stigma that the Silver Fire was a 'low priority' fire. Never mind that it was exhibiting the potential to become a monster fire. We had to plead, cajole and fight for our share of the limited resources available throughout the Western United States.

On September 16 at 1330 hours, I received a cryptic radio message from Incident Commander Dick Hodge. This is verbatim per my notes.

"The huge column of smoke coming out of the Silver and Indigo Creek area is the fire making a big run."

He went on. "It has jumped Indigo Creek, and we are evacuating the Janes family (a family on a small ranch on the edge of the forest). We are also pulling crews out of the Fishhook area. The logging crew is pulling out of Indigo."

The growing fire continued to make runs like that, gobbling up thousands of acres of forest each time. With continuing hot, dry weather and due to limited manpower and equipment, the strategy was to herd the fire from the flanks and not get anyone hurt.

The period of time from stepping into the office on the late afternoon of September 1, until the fire was finally contained on October 31 remains a hazy blur in my memory. I still have my 'Month at a Glance' appointment book and calendar from 1987, but it doesn't help much in reconstructing the events of those sixty days. Appointments scheduled long before the fire event had been scratched out and replaced with fire-related activities such as reviewing fire situation analysis and selecting suppression strategies for both the Silver and Longwood Fires, and with Wayne's assistance, briefing incoming suppression teams, and when the time came debriefing outgoing teams.

My job was to continue to be the forest supervisor and keep the normal functions of the forest operating. My primary role on the fires was to pass on my knowledge of the resources of the Siskiyou Forest and briefing incoming incident commanders about important or sensitive natural resources. Then discuss overall strategy and safety considerations. As time passed it seemed to me I was in a constant round of briefings and debriefings as fire teams were rotated about every two weeks on both the Silver and Longwood Fires.

I flew over the fires several times in both fixed-wing and helicopters with Wayne, and then briefed industry groups, environmental organizations, county commissioners and the media on the status of the fires and our suppression strategy. I also visited the large fire camps which were self-contained instant communities of nearly a thousand firefighters. I walked fire lines to converse with the ground troops and observe firsthand the fire conditions, suppression activity, safety practices and crew morale.

Looking for Lou

The Silver Fire had spread to the base of Bald Mountain and threatened to make a run to the top. Consideration was being given to dropping flares by helicopter and igniting backfires from the Illinois River, which lay just south of Bald Mountain. It was the only natural barrier to the fire spreading south. After a brief deliberation I decided against this tactic. Backfires often burn hotter than the fire itself, and the Illinois River canyon was just too precious a place to incinerate. Besides, there was a chance Lou Gold was in the area somewhere. I felt that if the fire spotted entirely across this steep, rocky canyon, the river environs might be spared, and down into the canyon would have been the logical line of retreat for Lou. If the fire crossed the river and headed south, so be it.

I was very concerned about Lou Gold. I had a feeling he might just be in the middle of all this! I made some inquires and learned he had, indeed, been camped atop Bald Mountain during the lightning storm, keeping watch over this, his revered place. I asked the IC for a favor, and he placed his chief scout and a helicopter at my disposal to see if we could find Lou and get him off the mountain.

However, that afternoon the fire made a major run up the

flanks of Bald Mountain to its very top. We had to delay our flight until the next morning. The fire had doubled in size to nearly 30,000 acres. We were able to land near the top and hiked to the area where I knew Lou had been camped. It was eerie. I knew this place well, but it was a burned-out shell of the former shaded, serene place it had been. No green trees, only blackened, still-smoking tree trunks and bared limbs.

I located his campsite and found melted clumps of aluminum, the remains of cooking utensils. Scattered pages of a partially burned copy of the draft Forest Plan were blowing in the light breeze. I picked up one charred page. Ironically, the page was entitled 'Wildfire Suppression'. I tucked it away in my cruiser vest. Lou was not there.

I presumed and hoped Lou had watched the fire activity increase at the base of the mountain, realized what might happen and left the mountaintop. I hoped that he had made his way down the steep, south side of the mountain to the Illinois River, from where he could hike upriver to the nearest road. This would be a tough way to walk out, but it was possible.

I learned a few days later that was what he had done. I was greatly relieved.

With little effective action being taken, the fire rapidly expanded through the rugged terrain of the unroaded and heavily vegetated Kalmiopsis Wilderness and became a conflagration. Following another major run the new IC, Gordon Rheinhart, reported:

> *The blow-up effect was just like opening the draft on a wood stove, when the oxygen reached the super-heated gases, they ignited explosively. The extreme fire behavior generated flames up to 400 feet in height.*

A couple of months later I was meeting with Lou Gold and a

few other environmentalists in my office to discuss the Silver Fire Recovery Plan. They were strongly opposed to any effort to salvage fire-killed timber. The recovery stage and project was on a course to be even more controversial and difficult than the fire itself.

Lou said something that has remained in my memory of this traumatic time. He said it seemed to him that: "The Supreme Being had declared a pox on both our houses, and perhaps the fire was a message to quit fighting over Bald Mountain and the North Kalmiopsis unroaded area and leave it in peace." That was not to be.

Fire and Politics

During the heat of the suppression campaign, in its early stages, forest products industry leaders, their paid representatives, and commissioners from both Josephine and Curry Counties were pressing me to authorize extending roads into the unroaded portions of the fire. The rationale was that it would offer better access for firefighting equipment and personnel. That was certainly true, but they were also thinking ahead to the timber salvage program that was sure to follow.

The leaders of local environmental groups were well aware of this point of view and rumors were flying. They were constantly calling me for information, demanding meetings, and expressing their adamant opposition to any and all road extensions. I tried to convince them we were respecting this roadless area, and I had no intention of pushing new roads into these areas to fight the fire. Nevertheless, they remained suspicious and apprehensive. *This borders on paranoia,* I thought. The calls and meeting demands kept coming, and were frankly becoming a major time consumer and distraction to the main priority – suppressing this fire.

Following a meeting with Headwaters, a very active environmental group operating out of Ashland, Oregon, I made a suggestion to their chairperson, Julie Norman. She was a tall, thin, intense young woman that I had found to be relatively open-minded, while remaining extremely dedicated to her cause.

"Julie," I asked, "how would you like to be assigned to the Silver Fire?"

She was startled and quickly replied, "What do you mean?"

"Well, Julie, I've hired hundreds of people in temporary firefighter and service positions on these fires, and I would like to hire one more."

"In what capacity?" she asked, and I saw a flicker of interest in her eyes.

"As an observer and direct liaison to the incident commander," I replied. "You could get a firsthand look at the fire, participate in fire suppression planning meetings, and represent the environmentalists' point of view to the IC."

She nodded and asked, "Why would you want me to do that?" (Did I mention she was also smart?)

"In addition," I said, "you could keep all the local environmental groups briefed and up to date on what is actually going on, and hopefully put an end to the rumor mill and speculation. That would be of great help to me." She agreed, and we went down the hall to personnel to sign her up.

My staff was surprised; industry leaders displeased, but the IC gracefully accepted the added complication. Following a period of shadowing the IC, being present at the daily briefing sessions, and seeing the fire and suppression action firsthand, Julie was satisfied we were not recklessly constructing roads, nor planning to do so. She also told me she had experienced all she needed of getting up at five a.m. and putting in fourteen-hour days. So by mutual agreement we ended her employment. Similar to the now common practice in our recent military conflicts, she was, to my knowledge, the first 'embedded' environmentalist and reporter in a major fire campaign. Probably the last too.

Julie and I crossed paths again at a memorial service for our well known and widely respected volunteer forest naturalist Mary Paetzel. The conversation eventually turned to the Silver Fire, and she asked me if I recalled the time I had hired her to work as an advisor to the Incident Commander of the Silver Fire. Of course I recalled the incident clearly. She laughed and said "I just wasn't used to getting up at 5 a.m. every morning for a briefing – and two weeks of that was entirely enough!"

The Silver Fire was declared 'contained' on October 31, but not declared out until the November rains finally arrived. It consumed 96,500 acres, about half of which was within the unroaded area north of the Kalmiopsis Wilderness, and half within the Wilderness itself. It had burned a swath ten miles wide from the Bear Camp Road near the Rogue River, and marched thirty-five miles south to just across the California state line.

The Galice Fire burned 21,000 acres, much of it on BLM land within the Rogue River canyon. Through mutual agreement the State of Oregon managed this fire suppression effort.

The Longwood Fire burned nearly 10,000 acres around the communities of Cave Junction and Takilma. These communities were home to many local environmental activists, and the fire was in their backyard. However, due to the high-profile unroaded area within the Silver Fire and the high stakes involved, it commanded the headlines. The Longwood fire, however, was actually a greater threat to people and communities. The district ranger at Cave Junction was Dennis Holthus, a quiet, unflappable and very effective manager and administrator. I relied heavily on 'Denny' to manage this fire suppression effort.

I was thankful and grateful to see these fires come to an end, but the drama had really just begun.

Fire Recovery and Timber Salvage

The Silver Fire had rekindled a long-standing land allocation disagreement over an extremely controversial unroaded area. The wood products industry saw the fire suppression effort and the potential salvage project as an opportunity to break the back of the roadless controversy by building roads to suppress the fire, and later utilize the roads to salvage the fire-killed timber. They pressured the Forest Service and local politicians, both privately and publicly, to build roads right now, during the confusion of the suppression effort.

On the other hand, the existing Bald Mountain road was the site of the first Earth First! road blockade – a shrine of sorts. They put me on notice they would do whatever it took to prevent further road construction. The balance of the more mainstream environmental community were determined to use the more conventional tactics of appeal and lawsuit to keep the area unroaded, and therefore suitable for classification as formal wilderness.

In the years prior to the fire, I had been pursuing my belief that the public stakeholders could resolve local issues in partnership with Forest Service people, with our role being one of facilitator and coach. I was determined to establish a new norm for solving public land problems and making decisions – a new social contract. I had enlisted the help of Bob Chadwick in this endeavor, and we had been successful in working through a few local issues with our local public. These, in a sense, had been only dress rehearsals; the curtain was about to rise on opening night of the principle drama.

Internally, I had also been working to make the transition of the forest leadership team to embrace a more participative management climate, and an open and flexible style with the capacity to move quickly. We tried to model this style for the entire forest. I believed that to be credible, this style must be congruent both internally and externally. The Silver Fire Recovery project would be a good test.

190

In order to succeed, the Silver Fire Recovery and salvage program would require an innovative organization, groundbreaking public involvement, and cutting-edge data and area analysis through a computer program called Geographic Information Systems or GIS. And finally to start the analysis process before the fire was even declared out.

We set up a separate, semi-independent group to analyze the fire effects, develop a recovery plan and prepare a Draft Environmental Impact Analysis. We designed a flat organization wherein great freedom to act independently was inherent, and minimal reviews were the norm. *Trust the people, trust the process*, I kept telling myself.

We put together a serendipitous blend of people who, together, were to make history. A board of directors that reported to me was headed by Timber Staff Officer John Hoffman. A tall, rangy, former smokejumper and district ranger, John had a sharp intellect and wasn't shy about unconventional approaches. I saw him as a visionary and strategist. The two district rangers involved, Terry DeGrow and Kathy Johnson, were comfortable with the freewheeling style of our design. Rich Stem, the project leader, possessed incredible energy and a prodigious capacity for work. He was also inclined to be an innovative risk taker and, perhaps best of all, had an irrepressible sense of humor. I could not have wished for more.

Stem approached me one morning and, somewhat hesitantly, proposed a series of public workshops with active and real hands-on citizen participation in weighing all the elements of the recovery plan, and together developing alternatives. He anxiously awaited my reaction. I was very pleased. "Exactly, right on!" I recall saying. Stem's proposal was right in line with the direction I wanted the forest to take. We began our public participation on January 25, 1988 with the first of a three-part Silver Fire Recovery Workshop held in the Riverside Inn Conference Center in downtown Grants Pass. About 150 people attended, representing the wood products industry, the environmental community, local government officials and, of course, the media.

We intended to break the assembly into more manageable workgroups, and we needed facilitators to work with each group. I borrowed a recognized expert in meeting facilitation from the regional office in Portland, and we spent a day training a group of forest employees on how to facilitate a group of strangers with opposing viewpoints to work together to produce a useful product.

We broke the large crowd into fifteen workgroups, being sure to get a mix of backgrounds and interests. The charge to each group was to develop a recovery and salvage alternative, but with each group assigned a theme or area of emphasis, such as watershed protection, or maximizing salvage volume, etc. All the subject matter experts on the Silver team were made available to them.

Following the last of these workshops, an article in the *Daily Courier* of January 30, 1988 summed it up best.

"Pro-timber industry folks sat next to staunch environmentalists Friday night during the final public involvement workshop ......while the factions didn't exactly embrace each other, observers noted there were no fistfights either."

The baseline alternatives the participants produced became the foundation the Silver team used in developing the DEIS.

I have struggled with how to capture the intensity, controversy and rapid change surrounding the event-filled episodes of that period of my watch over the Siskiyou Forest from September 1987 to June 1990. The effort to control the raging Silver and Longwood Fires, the following high-stakes salvage programs for the fire-killed timber, and the effort to simultaneously complete a final Forest Plan and EIS dominated the entire forest's workforce time and effort. I thought of it as trying to manage a three-ring circus!

There was also a headline-grabbing sideshow that was an effort of a few dedicated environmentalists to gain public and legislative support to convert the Siskiyou National Forest to a National Park. That way they would end road construction, timber harvest, mining and hunting in the Siskiyou forever. They did not get much support.

These events were high profile in Southwest Oregon, and occasionally in the entire state. Our progress was being closely monitored by Forest Service officials and legislators in Washington, D.C. The intensity was almost unbearable, the pace breathtaking, and controversy unprecedented. And it was unrelenting. So much living was crammed into those three years. I look back on it in awe that I survived. I had great help from a lot of good, committed Forest Service people. My evening jogs and occasional raft trips helped keep me sane.

The forest, the fires and salvage were often in the news. *The Grants Pass Daily Courier*, the *Medford Mail Tribune*, and the *Portland Oregonian* published a continuing stream of articles during that period. The Silver Fire and the following fire recovery process drew national attention. We were often on the front page, and likely sold lots of newspapers. The following is a sampling of those headlines:

The Silver Fire
"28,200 acre Silver Blaze Unattended" – Grants Pass Daily Courier 9/5/87

"Silver fire leaps over Illinois River" – Grants Pass Daily Courier 9/28/87

"Silver Fire largest ever in forest's history" – Grants Pass Daily Courier 9/24/87

"Fires made '87 a hellish nightmare" – Medford Mail Tribune 8/31/92

Silver Fire Recovery and Timber Salvage

"Logging fire-damaged timber kindles hot controversy" – Portland Oregonian 11/15/87

"Activists bloodied, but not beaten" – Grants Pass Daily Courier 6/23/88

"Logging compromise kindles anger" – Portland Oregonian 7/9/88

"Protesters return to Silver salvage area" – Grants Pass Daily Courier 8/3/88

"Supporters expanding (National) park proposal" – Grants Pass Daily Courier 12/16/88

"Forest fires and tempers flared in '87" – Grants Pass Daily Courier

Taken by themselves, the two large fires and their aftermath, all at the same time, would have been more than enough excitement for an entire career.

Bear Camp summit, smoke from the Silver Fire, 9/1/1987

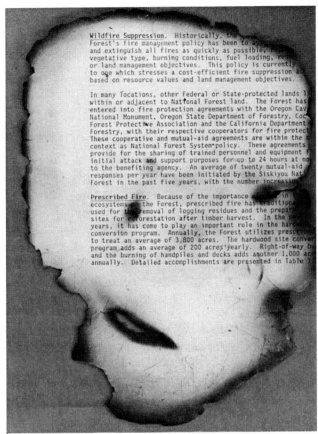

Charred page of the draft Forest Plan found on top of Bald Mountain

CHAPTER EIGHT

Conclusions

In late 1987, John Hoffman, Rich Stem and I, with the help of Regional Forester Jim Torrence, designed and assembled a Silver Fire recovery team of about sixty-five people. Some members originated from the Siskiyou, but most came from the other national forests of Oregon and Washington. The team and process were modeled after the 'Incident Command' system developed by the federal government to combat large forest fires and other natural disasters.

Help arrived from New Mexico, Utah, Minnesota, Montana, Nevada and California. These were folks with the specific skills we needed, including wildlife biologists, fisheries biologists, silviculturists, soil scientists, hydrologists, geologists, botanists, timber sale planners, logging system specialists, landscape architects, transportation planners, economists, archaeologists, and forest fuels specialists. They were all on loan; most came willingly, and some initially a bit grudgingly. All had full-time jobs and responsibilities on their forests of origin.

This process for a fire recovery, timber salvage and rehabilitation project was unprecedented in the history of the U.S. Forest Service. The time line established by Washington, D.C. to complete the public participation, planning and Environmental Impact Statement (EIS) was brutal. We had a target to produce a recovery plan and draft (DEIS) by mid-March of 1988 – six months!

The Silver Team

We formed a steering committee of John Hoffman, Rich Stem, and District Rangers Kathy Johnson and Terry DeGrow to lead the effort and keep key players briefed on an ongoing basis. It wasn't long before the project assumed a life of its own. The pace was breathtaking. The effort was characterized by running into problems and barriers, solving or finding a way around them, then developing original approaches and creative solutions. I became more facilitator/expediter than leader. I tried not to get in the way and supported the effort by pulling strings and calling in favors by acquiring personnel and equipment when needed.

This was all fine by me. In fact, I felt I was living an organizational dream. We had created a self-motivated, high-powered performance machine that was headed toward a mutually agreed upon goal. What more could a leader ask or hope for?

I frequently counseled myself, *Trust the people, trust the process, don't over control this, don't mess this up!*

The reason for the extraordinary high profile of this event was the long-smoldering issue of the North Kalmiopsis roadless area now reignited as a result of the Silver Fire, and the high volume of fire-killed timber within it. The Silver Fire brought this issue to a head and became a surrogate for similar roadless/timber issues across the United States.

In the meantime, Bob Ettner and his planning crew were striving to keep the Forest Land and Resource Management Plan on track, aiming to produce a DEIS on our target date for late 1988. These twin efforts dominated 1988. Completing the Forest Plan was a goal I was not willing to set aside.

Silver Briefings, Washington, D.C.

On January 21 and 22, 1988, John Hoffman, Rich Stem, Terry DeGrow and I were in Washington, D.C. to brief the congressional delegation from Oregon on the status of the recovery planning. This included Congressmen DeFazio and Smith, and Senators Hatfield and Packwood. We wanted to keep them informed and supportive of our effort.

We also briefed the national representatives of and attorneys for the timber industry, including the National Forest Products Association. We met with the national leaders of the principle environmental groups, including the Sierra Club, Wilderness Society and National Wildlife Federation, to name but a few. We created an outline of our presentation, and each of us presented a piece of the story, using maps, charts, and other visual aids. Then we responded to questions. We scheduled and conducted briefings all day and through the evenings for two days.

Part of Terry's presentation was to discuss our public participation process, and he described it as doing the planning in a 'fish bowl'. Rich had always thought the analogy was comical (who were the sharks, and who were the guppies?) and kidded Terry about it.

During the presentations to all these important people, Rich would look at Terry and smirk and try to conceal his grin. It was contagious, and John and I would work hard to suppress the urge to laugh out loud. Terry would smile patiently at Rich and go on with his presentation. Rich's sense of humor was a great asset; it relieved tension and tended to counter my sometimes overly serious demeanor.

We had an informative and slick presentation, and I am sure we left the impression that we were competent and committed – and we were. I closed the briefings by summarizing the process saying: "This is a very controversial area, with sensitive resources on extremely steep and difficult terrain. We are sincere in and committed to engaging the public as participants and partners in the planning process. We are intent on doing a first-class job of land stewardship here, and we are proceeding at top speed."

We returned to Grants Pass over the weekend. On Monday evening, January 25, 1988, we held the first of our Silver Recovery Public Workshops at the conference center of the Riverside Inn. The same night, incidentally, as President Reagan was to deliver his final State of the Union Address of his tenure as president. We drew a full house. I was sure the president did also.

'Bobcat' and Julie participated in the workshops and often visited me in my office concerning both the Silver Recovery Project and the Forest Plan. They were as committed as ever in defending the North Kalmiopsis roadless area and old-growth forests. I granted them access, just as I did to timber industry representatives.

In April of 1988, I was requested to return to Washington, D.C. and testify to the Subcommittee on Forests, Family Farms and Energy of the U.S. House of Representatives. They wanted firsthand information on our progress in bringing this timber salvage project on line. My role was to assist Deputy Chief George Leonard, who would have the lead in providing testimony and answering questions.

Typically, people who are asked to come in from the 'field' to testify are treated well and with respect. The legislators apparently feel for once they are going to receive the unvarnished truth on how things are out in the hinterlands.

Congressman Bob Smith, representing the Second Congressional District of Southern Oregon was a member of the committee.

The event was held in Room 1300 in the Longworth House Office Building. As I entered the room I was surprised to find a packed house. Every available seat was taken. I looked around the room and saw timber industry and forest product representatives from the Pacific Northwest, and also leading environmental group representatives. The same group of protagonists I had been working with back home for the past several years. It dawned on me that this was not going to be so much a fact-finding hearing as it was a 'show'.

Nevertheless, I felt confident and well prepared. I would be a credible witness. Following his introductory statement, George Leonard asked me to brief the subcommittee on the Silver Fire salvage situation. I presented a concise overview of the process we used, with the public's help, to prepare alternatives for a DEIS, the issues involved, and the amount of timber we were likely to salvage. I provided the members with photos of the fire area and information depicting the rate of deterioration of the fire-killed trees. I made the point that we must move quickly before these trees deteriorated to the point of marginal value. All in all, I thought it went well.

Then the question and answer period began. It was clear to me from the outset that the timber industry representatives had provided pointed questions to subcommittee members to ask both George and me. That is just the way these hearings work. They were, in part, conducting legitimate fact finding, and in part playing to their constituents and the media.

The following is transcribed verbatim from the Congressional Record, dated April 13, 1988. My thoughts and comments are in italics.

HEARING before the Subcommittee on Forests, Family Farms, and Energy of the Committee on Agriculture

House of Representatives

April 13, 1988

The Chairman of the Subcommittee, Mr. Volkmer of Missouri, asked me to review and summarize the recovery process following the Silver Fire, which I did. Then Congressman Robert F. Smith of Oregon began the questioning of both George and me. George handled the

questions in his usual very competent and articulate manner. Then it was my turn.

Mr. Leonard, ...environmental groups blame Senator Mark Hatfield, Au Coin and others in Congress for pressuring the Forest Service to cut more than it will grow. Is that a true statement?

Mr. Leonard: It is not.

Mr. Smith: Can I, as a Member of Congress, get your job?

Mr. Leonard: I hope not.

Mr. Smith: Mr. McCormick, can I get your job?

Mr. McCormick: I am not sure you would want it.

(Laughter)

Mr. Smith: Probably not today. No, I mean physically. Can I as a Member of Congress somehow get you fired?

Mr. McCormick: No.

I was trying to inject a little humor into this formal and tense atmosphere, but I could tell Congressman Smith did not appreciate my response. But George understood where Congressman Smith was going with this line of seemingly irrelevant questions, and he added the following:

Mr. Leonard: It is important to understand that we know of the interest of the Oregon and Washington delegation in producing timber.

Mr. Smith: Sure.

Mr. Leonard: And we take that into consideration because you, as elected officials, represent a very good cross section. It is one of the best indications we have of what the public opinion of a State or area is, what the elected officials want.

George and I answered a series of questions from other committee members from other states. They asked good questions with the intent of learning more about the facts of salvaging timber and rehabilitating the fire-damaged area, the EIS process, and the appeal process that was sure to follow.

It was Mr. Smith's turn again with a more provocative, and obviously a planted line of questioning.

Mr. Smith: You Mr. McCormick had an involvement with the Port-Orford-cedar consensus program in Oregon. Tell me about that and why didn't that consensus culminate in an agreement? I understand that was a year ago, and I understand that was a consensus program with ONRC. (Oregon Natural Resources Council)

Mr. McCormick: Not an agreement as such. I believe it was successful as far as it went. We received a letter from the Oregon Natural Resources Council, it has been two to three years ago now, that was prepared in the way of a legal brief, that pointed out that Port-Orford-cedar had a disease, root rot disease, that we had not taken much action to control, and that unless we were more vigorous in our approach to controlling that disease, we were going to end up in court regarding our harvest of Port-Orford-cedar.

As an alternative to court, I suggested to the group that we sit down and see if we could work out our differences. You can call it a consensus group or a problem-solving group, the term is not important to me. What was important was that we could mutually seek some solutions to what was really a mutual problem. Their concern over the fate of the cedar was ours also. And we did that. We developed a number of procedures together that we have implemented in our approach to sales now that have Port-Orford-cedar in them, and we have a number of guidelines that the districts, all the districts on the Siskiyou Forest, use regarding harvest of timber with Port-Orford-cedar in it, and we are not in court. So, from that standpoint, I see it as successful.

Mr. Smith: How far do you go, Mr. Chamberlain, to stay out of court? Never mind.

That stung!

Congressman Smith had evened the score for my previous flippant remark about him not wanting my job, and he struck a blow for the timber industry that continued to detest 'consensus seeking'. He had made it clear to all that he felt recognizing environmental groups as a legitimate member of the public, and working with them, was 'appeasement'.

It was a cheap shot and I wanted to respond. I turned to George for the go ahead, but he shook his head, no.

The reference to 'Mr. Chamberlain', of course, was to the British Prime Minister Neville Chamberlain, who, in the years leading up to World War II (1937-1940) attempted to appease Nazi Germany by agreeing, along with France and Italy, to cede a portion of German-speaking Czechoslovakia to Germany as a measure to avoid war at any cost. History now views his attempts at appeasement as a tragic blunder and has judged Mr. Chamberlain as a weak prime minister and a failure.

A few more questions followed, and then we were excused. The next witness was Andy Kerr, director of the Oregon Natural Resources Council. We left the hearing room and I did not hear Mr. Kerr's testimony. I thought it interesting that the subcommittee wanted to hear his viewpoint.

I believed then, as I do now, that resolution of public land and resource issues can best be achieved 'on the ground'. That is, locally, with all the protagonists involved. Participative problem solving and consensus seeking remain my preferred choice over the alternatives of appeals, lawsuits, and legislative 'riders'.

The End of the Road

The most contentious issue surrounding the salvage of the timber killed by the Silver Fire was the extension of the now infamous Bald Mountain Road. Previous construction had been halted by a court-ordered preliminary injunction issued in July of 1983. Work had stopped immediately on a steep, heavily forested hillside. This was an impossible location to construct a place to enable a helicopter carrying logs picked up from the fire area and suspended from cables to place them near trucks for loading. This required an open area at least a quarter acre of relatively flat ground to accommodate a deck of logs, room for a logging truck turn around, and loading equipment to operate. In timber jargon such an area is simply called a 'landing'.

The Bald Mountain Road and this northern area of the huge fire were within the Fourth Congressional District of a relatively new congressman, Peter DeFazio. A Democrat, he had been elected to his first term in 1988. His staff had been in contact with me on a regular basis since the initiation of the fire recovery and timber salvage planning. His field office was located in Eugene, the home of the University of Oregon. Students and environmentalists were a significant part of his constituency.

The question posed to me by DeFazio's staff was: "How much salvage timber would be available without extending the Bald Mountain Road?" The short answer was little or none. The near impossibility of constructing a landing at the present end of the road, and the limited range of a helicopter carrying a load of logs, made this clear.

The staff of Oregon's long-serving senator, Republican Mark Hatfield, had also been in constant contact. Senator Hatfield's support came from the timber industry. Tall and lean with graying hair, he looked every bit a senator. I had found him to be a bright, straightforward man, and a statesman. He was the timber industry's 'go to' person when they needed political support and legislative intervention.

If we were to have a politically acceptable solution to salvaging the fire-killed timber, I knew it would be necessary to have the support of both Congressman DeFazio and Senator Hatfield.

I had asked the forest logging engineer to identify alternative landings that would put the helicopters within economical range of the fire-killed timber but minimize the distance of an extension of the Bald Mountain Road. He concluded that an extension of the road of at least one half-mile would be required to reach the closest suitable landing site. One half-mile doesn't sound like much, but to the environmental community it would be viewed with alarm. It was May of 1988. I called Congressman DeFazio's staff and invited the congressman to join me and walk the proposed road extension to the proposed landing.

The next day the call was returned by a staff representative. "The congressman will do it on the condition there is no press, and no additional Forest Service people involved."

I pondered this for a minute and finally replied, "I can agree to that." We set a date and time to meet.

He brought along one staff person, which I expected. Congressman Peter DeFazio and I shook hands and sized each other up. I saw a short, bespectacled, balding man with a mustache. He was not a commanding physical figure, but he appeared fit. Looking into his eyes I had the impression of a sharp intellect. His demeanor was quiet and informal as he, in turn, sized me up. Based on only a first impression, I recall thinking to myself, *I believe I can trust and work with this new congressman.*

"Let's hike the road location to the closest feasible helicopter landing site we have identified," I proposed. "It is cross country and a little rough, but it's less than a mile."

The congressman smiled faintly and agreed.

The survey crew had 'brushed out' a trail along the proposed route, and Mr. DeFazio appeared to be in good shape and had no trouble negotiating the steep hillside. My respect for the man grew.

We took our time, and his staff person made notes and took photographs.

About an hour later we arrived at the top of a rounded hill that would be the acceptable helicopter landing area that our logging engineer had identified. I turned to Mr. DeFazio and asked, "Well, what do you think?"

He paused only for a moment and said, "I don't have a personal problem with extending the road to this point." Then added, "But I am not confident that the environmental organizations will accept it."

In the days that followed there was a flurry of activity in the offices of both Congressman DeFazio and Senator Hatfield. The congressman put together a proposal extending the Bald Mountain Road about one half-mile to the proposed landing. He also included withdrawing or deferring the unroaded area from future timber harvest following the salvage logging of fire- killed timber. The latter measure was an inducement for the environmental community to support the proposal. Something for everyone, or so it seemed.

If the environmental community rejected the proposal and went forward with a lawsuit and a request for a preliminary injunction to stop the salvage logging, Senator Hatfield was prepared to add an amendment or 'rider' to the upcoming appropriations bill to preclude lawsuits on salvage logging of the Silver Fire.

Not to be without a plan of our own, our strategy was to forge ahead as quickly as possible with the FEIS, and cause the industry, the environmentalists and politicians to have to scramble to keep up. I felt we could keep ahead of everyone.

We were about to issue the FEIS, when, on July 8, 1988, the National Wildlife Federation and Earth First! jointly filed a motion for a temporary restraining order enjoining the Forest Service from building the road extension or offering the fire-killed timber for sale. The plaintiffs' complaint was that we had prepared an inadequate FEIS. A hearing was set for July 21 in a federal court in Portland.

Of course, most everyone outside of the Siskiyou Forest thought we would lose the court proceeding and the injunction would be granted. That had been the recent history of lawsuits by environmentalists against the Forest Service across the country. We thought differently.

We knew we had prepared an excellent FEIS and had involved our publics every step along the way. We also knew we had selected a very reasonable and moderate salvage alternative, including a minimal extension of the Bald Mountain Road. We would salvage much of the fire-killed timber, but by helicopter, thereby limiting ground-disturbing activity. Our plan just made good sense. And we had a cadre of experts who had prepared the recovery plan and FEIS. They would be excellent witnesses.

In spite of full participation by local representatives, the principle environmental organizations rejected our plan and FEIS. I was not surprised, but I was disappointed. No road building and no tree cutting (even dead trees) was their mantra. One prominent environmentalist had coined the phrase, "Cutting these trees would be like raping a burn victim." There was just no 'give' in most of those folks, particularly at the national level of their respective organizations.

However, we were prepared, confident, and even eager to present our case.

At the hearing in the federal courthouse in Portland, we paraded our cadre of subject matter expert witnesses for testimony in front of the judge. They did very well, obviously professional, knowledgeable and committed. Just before lunch, the plaintiffs' attorney asked the judge to put me on the stand. I had a momentary flash of panic, as I was not on the witness list and was not prepared to testify. My staff laughed and enjoyed my discomfort. Rich Stem grinned at me as only he could. I thought that the ability to laugh and enjoy some humor during these tense proceedings was a good sign – even if it was at my expense. Mercifully, the judge said there had been enough witnesses, and my testimony would not be necessary.

The judge issued his ruling the next day. It read in part, "To earn a preliminary injunction the moving party must demonstrate either a combination of probable success and the possibility of irreparable injury or that serious questions are raised and the balance of hardships tips sharply in its favor... Because the FEIS is clearly adequate and, in my judgment, passes the test described above, I rule here for the defendants. The plaintiffs' motion for a preliminary injunction is DENIED." We had won the first skirmish!

The Rider from Hell

Since the National Wildlife Federation had filed the notion for a preliminary injunction, and because most observers including the timber industry expected the Forest Service to lose and be enjoined from proceeding (as had been the recent history), Senator Hatfield had been persuaded to attach an amendment or rider to that year's appropriation bill which precluded injunctions or lawsuits on timber salvage FEIS and projects. This was termed 'sufficiency language' and meant the EIS would not be subject to judicial review. It was a 'failsafe' action by the timber industry. The environmentalists called it 'the rider from hell'.

The timber industry still wanted it all – to build the road into the heart of the area, end the 'roadless' classification, and harvest all of the fire-killed timber. 'Cut every black stick' became their slogan. The appropriation bill for most government agencies, which included Senator Hatfield's rider, was signed into law shortly after we prevailed in the lawsuit for preliminary injunction. I was disappointed. We had just demonstrated we had a viable project and a sound FEIS, and we didn't need, however well intentioned, political intervention. I felt it reduced the significance of our effort and increased the bitterness and resolve of the environmental community.

Winning this initial lawsuit was big news in the Forest Service and drew a lot of attention. A review of the Silver project by an analyst out of the Portland regional office concluded in her December 1988 publication:

> *The Silver organization was a performance machine. Unbelievable workloads were met with a dynamic forged of excitement, creativity, sheer hard work, and hours that would make even a diehard workaholic stagger. The atmosphere was electric: charged minds bent to the task, determined to accomplish it...*

This extraordinary effort by the cadre of regular Forest Service people who worked night and day to produce a high-quality Fire Recovery Plan and EIS in record time still stands as a monumental achievement that I don't believe has been matched to this day. The Forest Service and particularly the Siskiyou National Forest projected an image of a credible, first-class organization that can get the job done.

The temporary office was closed down and team members returned to their respective forests. If you were part of the Silver Fire Recovery Project, I know you will never forget the experience, and you earned the right to be proud of your involvement.

The project went forward, and 136 million board feet of blackened trees were harvested by helicopter with minimal damage to soils and fish habitat. Thousands of new trees were quickly planted in the most severely burned areas.

The Forest Plan

We had issued the Proposed Land and Resource Management Plan (Forest Plan) and Draft EIS in August 1987, just before the

Silver Fire. The fire and the recovery planning, EIS and court injunction slowed but did not stop the forest planning process.

In late 1988 we made the transition from the Silver Fire Recovery Project to once again focusing on finishing the Forest Plan and final EIS. No national forest in Oregon west of the Cascade Mountains had yet published a Forest Plan. Even with the setback and delay caused by the Silver Fire and recovery, we were still in a position to lead the region and be one of the first to publish.

'Bobcat' and Julie were still busy tracking our plan process and continued to periodically visit with me and Bob Ettner with questions and ideas. I gave them high marks for commitment.

By the end of 1988, we were nearly ready to publish the final Forest Plan and EIS. I had a few hurdles to clear first. I was required to brief the chief and his staff in Washington, D.C. to get final clearance to publish. Everett Towle, my former forest supervisor on the Inyo Forest, and now director of planning in the Washington office, had invited me to stay with him and his wife, Arlene, at their home just outside of Washington, D.C. Ev had always been a supporter and good friend. I flew to Washington on Sunday, November 6, 1988.

Washington, D.C. – Again

There was always something heady and exciting about traveling to Washington on official business. I was there again, at the seat of power, wearing suit and tie, and carrying a briefcase across the mall in the capitol of the United States of America.

I was scheduled to brief the chief of the Forest Service and his principle staff on Monday afternoon. The forest supervisors of the Coleville and Malheur National Forests were also there for a similar briefing.

When my turn came I was a bit nervous, as always, but confident we had produced a good plan; one that balanced the considerable resources and values of the Siskiyou in a way that made good sense. Ev was sitting in the row of deputy chiefs and staff just behind Chief Dale Robertson. I looked at Ev for reassurance. He smiled and nodded.

I made my presentation, hitting these high points:

"Chief Robertson, we had 17,000 individual public responses to the draft plan and DEIS. Seventeen thousand!"

It was clear there was great interest in this first plan for a national forest with both heavy timber volumes and large unroaded areas to be published. I don't know if any plan in the country received as many responses.

I continued, "Our district rangers and planning team have concluded, based on public response and resource analysis, that the key or distinctive values of the forest are: the capacity to grow timber, the spawning and juvenile rearing habitat for salmon and steelhead, the rich botanical and biological diversity, the major rivers – the Rogue, Illinois, Chetco and Elk, and the nearly 300,000 acres of unroaded area."

This is an over-simplified summary of a complicated planning process. But in summary I posited that in order to protect and perpetuate all these values and provide a more balanced plan, we needed to place more emphasis on fish habitat, wildlife habitat and ecological values, and reduce the timber harvest accordingly.

I described the acres we proposed to designate for wildlife and fisheries habitat, thereby reducing the acres available for timber harvest.

The chief was frowning. When it came time for the questions, the chief challenged our reasons for taking acres out of the timber base, such as the large acreage set aside for the spotted owl habitat, the proposed drop in the annual sale quantity, and other timber-related questions. Nothing was asked about fisheries habitat, wildlife, watershed protection, recreation management, or ecosystem perpetuation.

What happened to balance and 'multiple-use', I wondered? But it was clear I dared not ask. I was more than disappointed.

Everett had observed and sensed my disillusionment and later counseled me.

"Ron, you have to realize we are in an administration with an Assistant Secretary of Agriculture dedicated to increasing, not decreasing the timber cut from the national forests. The chief was politically obligated to ask those questions."

"Yes, I guess I understand, but that doesn't make it right. This is one hell of a way to manage the nation's natural resources."

To my surprise, the chief did approve our proposed final plan, and sanctioned the forest to publish it and the Final Environmental Impact Statement.

Back Home

I returned home to Oregon and began a constant round of briefings for leaders of the environmental community, including Julie Norman of Headwaters, Andy Kerr of Oregon Natural Resources Council, timber industry representatives, state officials including the Oregon Department of Fish and Wildlife, the governor's personal representative assigned to forest planning, and staff representatives to Oregon's congressional delegation. I also briefed the editorial boards of the Grants Pass, Medford and Portland newspapers.

I didn't want any group or individual to be surprised, and I wanted our interest groups and media fully informed on where we were headed with the plan. I still intended to reduce the forest's annual sale quantity of timber to be sold annually by at least fifteen percent.

The timber industry was well aware of our intent, and that of other forests in Western Oregon. They organized a meeting at the Sun River Resort near Bend, Oregon. All the timber industry representatives were to attend, and all the forest supervisors and the regional forester were invited to attend. The subject was the forest planning process.

On the first evening, a key industry representative cornered me during the cocktail hour. He was the same one who led the attack on me that first meeting a few years previous in Grants Pass. He told me flat out. "We will never let you publish *that* plan," then he smirked and walked away.

I pondered his statement. *What did he know that I didn't?*

Our draft Forest Plan and EIS had proposed to reduce the timber offered for sale annually from the 180 million board feet, which we had been averaging the past few years, to 150 million board feet. I intended to hold to that number.

One afternoon on the eve of publishing the plan, I received a call from the regional forester. He had been on the phone with the governor of Oregon, who told him he could not live with such a reduction and asked that the final plan and EIS reflect an ASQ in the mid-160s. Apparently the governor had made some election campaign promises to the industry. I argued the point, but it was clear the regional forester felt he had to placate the governor. We debated a bit more and agreed on a compromise of 160 million board feet. The regional forester said he would try to get the governor to accept it. It was more political meddling from an unexpected source. The industry representatives had earned their pay.

The plan and FEIS were published on March 15, 1989, the first of the Western Oregon national forests to complete a plan under the requirements of the 1976 National Forest Management Act.

In spite of the last-minute political intervention, we received generally positive reviews from the media. I believe the contacts with the editorial boards of all the local area and Portland papers, and our intensive public involvement effort, paid dividends. In addition, the district rangers of the coastal side of the forest, Mike Frazier and Kathy Johnson, did very well in their interviews with local reporters.

The following is a sampling of editorials and articles:

"Siskiyou plan details new forest management strategy" – Curry Costal Pilot, Gold Beach, 3/15/89

"New forest management plan shaves back timber sales" – The Oregonian, Portland, 3/15/89

"Siskiyou plan walks line" – Grants Pass Daily Courier, 3/15/89

"Plan draws predictable praise, criticism" – Grants Pass Daily Courier, 3/15/89

"Siskiyou plan sets the pace for the future" – Editorial, Grants Pass Daily Courier, 3/18/89

"Governor backs plan for forest" *(Imagine that)* – The Daily Tidings, Ashland, 3/15/89

"Environmentalists challenge Siskiyou plan" – Grants Pass Daily Courier, 6/27/89

The plan eventually received six appeals: five from environmental organizations and one from the timber industry. No surprises there.

Under the circumstances I felt we did the best we could to achieve a sound Forest Plan for the Siskiyou National Forest.

New Forestry and the Shasta Costa Endeavor

Dr. Jerry Franklin was a plant ecologist at the Forest Service Pacific Northwest Research Station, and a Professor of Ecosystem Analysis at the University of Washington. Dr. Franklin had been working for several years on alternative approaches to maintaining biological diversity and ecological integrity in forests while extracting wood products.

He approached the problem on a landscape, as opposed to a project level. He had become a beacon of hope and a guiding light to those in the Forest Service interested in alternative approaches to timber harvest.

Dr. Franklin had coined the term 'New Forestry' for his revolutionary concepts.

Jerry was fast attaining 'guru' status, but he was a controversial figure within the Forest Service, both admired and detested depending on one's mindset. The environmental community idolized him, but the timber industry was very wary and suspicious. One industry representative quipped prophetically, "Maybe New Forestry is better than no forestry at all."

To his credit, Chief Dale Robertson legitimized the concept. The Washington office produced a brochure, *New Perspectives: An Ecological Path for Managing Forests.*

I was acquainted with Jerry and admired his early work. At the urging of District Ranger Pete Broast, I took the entire management team to the H. J. Andrews Experimental Forest near Eugene, Oregon so we could see firsthand some of the on-the-ground demonstrations of these concepts.

The main components of the concept were:

1. Plan wood products extractions within the larger context of the landscape.
2. Leave and maintain 'course woody debris' – snags and down logs.
3. Leave groups of green trees within harvest areas.
4. Create tree and shrub stands of mixed species and a multi-layered canopy structure.
5. Minimize the fragmenting of old growth stands into tiny blocks.

These concepts fit my notion of a modern ecosystem-based forestry. I liked what I saw at H. J. Andrews, and so did the district rangers and staff.

At the time, many of the unroaded areas on the Siskiyou had been determined not suitable for inclusion into the Wilderness system and, therefore by default, made part of the 'timber base' available for future timber sales. In addition, by direction and mandate from on high, all of this category of land had been and was still being used to calculate the ASQ of the forest, our protestations to the contrary. To date we had not entered any of these unroaded lands. The balance of the suitable timbered lands on the forest was absorbing the difference and one of the many reasons for a continued inappropriately high ASQ.

We embraced the concepts of 'new forestry', and in the style of the Siskiyou decided to run with it. The Shasta Costa Project was born, and we were in the lead again in the Pacific Northwest Region with a 'cutting edge' project – just where I wanted us to be. The best part about it was that I didn't need to encourage this new endeavor. I just unleashed the energy and commitment of the people of the Siskiyou.

Timber Staff Officer John Hoffman analyzed our options and recommended the Shasta Costa drainage, lying mostly on the Gold Beach Ranger District, as our best opportunity.

We invited Dr. Franklin to visit the Shasta Costa Project on the ground and view the landscape via aircraft. We wanted his ideas and support. He was gratified that someone was listening to him. We put together a special team on the forest and went to work.

Our concept was to take participative management one step further and have both timber industry and environmental representatives be a part of the planning team. We were sincere in this commitment, seeing it as the way of the future.

This story, for me, had a sad ending for which I bear the primary responsibility. Changes in key personnel, dramatic events in the old growth and spotted owl national arena, and the passage of time worked against this wonderful project. It was conceived in the heat of idealistic fervor and born full of excitement and hope.

The forest published an innovative brochure, and the DEIS came out in mid-1990. But the FEIS and plan did not emerge from the morass of the engulfing old growth and spotted owl controversy until mid-1996! In the ensuing years most of the main players on the Siskiyou had either retired or moved on. And the final product only faintly resembled the project as originally envisioned. The environmental community felt betrayed.

I believe we dithered away a wonderful opportunity to design a way to manage forest resources using ecological approaches, and even more importantly, engaging former protagonists as partners. Utopian, perhaps, but possible nonetheless. For the doubters out there, our hearts were true.

The Spotted Owl and the Northwest Forest Plan

In late 1989 and early 1990, three monumental events unfolded in rapid succession that completely overshadowed, some might say negated, much of the local forest planning work:

1. The Report of Scientists on Spotted Owl Habitat led by Jack Ward Thomas and published in April 1990. *The Interagency Scientific Committee Report Summary* of April 4, 1990 stated that the new strategy "...largely abandons the current and, we believe, flawed system...in favor of protecting larger blocks of habitat – which we term Habitat Conservation Areas or HCAs."

2. Listing the spotted owl as a threatened species by the U.S. Fish and Wildlife Service on June 23, 1990.

3. Finally and conclusively, the Timber Summit held in Portland, Oregon, and the ensuing Northwest Forest Plan. This process was personally led by President Bill Clinton and Vice President Al Gore. It was completed in July 1993.

The report to Congress on this plan dated July 16, 1993 by the Congressional Research Service stated:

On April 2, 1993 President Clinton fulfilled a campaign promise by convening a forest conference in Portland, OR, to address the gridlock over management of the Federal forest lands in the Pacific Northwest and the resulting effects on communities and the regional economy.

In summary, the essence of this plan was to set aside huge 'Reserve Areas' within national forest and BLM lands for spotted owl habitat, where very limited management activities could occur. And it set aside nearly as large 'Adaptive Management Areas' where research and experimentation could occur.

The net effect was to significantly reduce the timber harvest on Pacific Northwest public lands. On the Siskiyou National Forest this worked out to a reduction from the 160 million board feet annual sale quantity to something less than twenty-five million. Wow! Who could have guessed?

In my humble opinion, the pendulum had swung in the other direction far past the point of balance.

After I had been on the Siskiyou for a while and began to know the forest well, it became clear to me that the nearly 180 million board feet current timber sale level was high – too high to sustain over time. The district rangers confirmed that their assessment for their ranger district was similar. Our data and analysis supported that conclusion.

I wondered how we got to this level of harvest. I found it was for reasons both internal and external.

A legacy of World War II was the cry from Congress to increase the harvest from public lands to meet the demand for housing for returning veterans. It was a clear mandate with public support. The Forest Service responded magnificently and received both kudos and increased funding from Congress. Our reputation as a 'can-do' outfit was born and institutionalized in our culture.

The timber management planning process had some assumptions built into the computer formulas designed to calculate tree growth rates and sustainable production. The forecast for success of plantations, fertilization to increase rates of growth, reduction of competition by tree thinning and brush removal, were all optimistic. The reality was proving to be less than optimal. In addition, as mentioned in my painful reiteration of the Shasta Costa Project, we were required to calculate the ASQ as if the unroaded areas were available for timber sale projects – which in reality they were not.

Combine these factors with a then powerful timber industry, and the periodic pressure or direction by the administration and congress to increase the volume advertised for sale to bolster the economy during recessions, and you can see how we got to the high harvest levels.

In the natural world, over reactions and out-of-balance situations are usually remedied with an equal and opposite reaction. Environmental organizations and individuals watched the evolution of the Forest Service unfold and were appalled. In part it was one of the events that sparked the ascendancy of the environmental movement in the 1970s and 1980s. They became skillful in the use of the appeals system under federal regulation and the National Environmental Policy Act. The situation reversed course and powered ahead in another direction, and we arrived at stalemate.

Now, I believe we have gone too far in the other direction, and my rationale is simple. As a nation we continue to build homes and shopping centers as fast as ever. From where will the wood products come, and under what environmental constraints will the trees be harvested? Anecdotal information coming from Canada, South America, Russia and elsewhere suggests constraints are minimal or nonexistent. When I take a global perspective and ask myself, is the earth and its ecosystem better off if the public lands of the United States are, for all practical purposes, 'off-limits' to timber harvest? My answer is, I think not.

In a global context, the United States of America cannot be

selfish. NIOBY (not in our back yard) is in a global ecological sense totally inappropriate. I know full well the products will come from somewhere else under minimal extraction constraints. The result will be more damage and harm to global ecosystems. I believe the USA needs to provide its fair share, but lead the world with enlightened, professional management practices.

I believe in the United States that public land management agencies know how to manage land and harvest trees and extract other natural resources thoughtfully, with care and an eye to the future. If not us, then who else on our troubled earth?

Lest I be overly negative here, these developments did not negate all of the very good forest management decisions and allocations made in the Siskiyou Plan, of which we were all very proud:

- We identified and added nineteen new Botanical Areas to the three already existing.
- We added four additional Research Natural Areas to the four existing.
- We identified and set aside 153 one-thousand-acre spotted owl areas.
- We created 'back-country recreation' areas of 41,000 acres.
- We reserved and protected 180,000 acres of old-growth trees.
- We refined and improved the standards and guidelines for protecting and managing all of the forest's resources.
- And we reduced the timber harvest. Not enough in my judgment, but the best we could do given the political circumstances.

Last Official Visit to Washington, D.C.

In mid-1989 I was called back to Washington one final time. I invited Carol and Trina to accompany me. The purpose of the trip was to receive a Superior Service Award from the Secretary of Agriculture. This was a unit award to the Siskiyou National Forest for the Silver Fire suppression and resource recovery accomplishments. The citation read: "For extraordinary leadership and resource recovery accomplishment...." I accepted it on behalf of all the employees of the Siskiyou.

On the flight home I thought about the recognition the forest had received, and of my five-part 'Vision for the Forest' statement I had presented to my management team in that pivotal February 1984 team-building session at Steamboat (see Chapter 6). It read, in part:

"The Siskiyou develops and maintains a reputation as a forest that develops future leaders in the Forest Service. It becomes known as a good, exciting, progressive forest that nurtures its employees. It's *the* place to be."

I was satisfied that together we had more than achieved that vision. During my watch of seven years, I had done the best I could for the Siskiyou National Forest and our employees.

There was a freight train loaded with yet more apocalyptic change that continued to rumble our way. I was out of breath, bruised and tired. An infusion of fresh energy was going to be required, and I sensed it was time to hand off the responsibility of caring for the Siskiyou National Forest, nurturing its employees and serving the people, to a successor.

I had experienced thirty-three years with the U.S. Forest Service. It had always been interesting, demanding, and at times almost too exciting. I was blessed with the good fortune to work for the best federal agency of the time, and with the greatest generation of U.S. Forest Service people in the history of the agency. I was fulfilled.

I decided to retire, and did so June 1, 1990.

Ron, I really appreciate the great job your doing on the Siskiyou NF! Keep up the good work! F. Dale Robertson Chief

Dale Robertson, Chief of the Forest Service in Washington, D.C.

Letters

USFS' Ron McCormick will be sorely missed

You can count on one hand the number of major players in the timber debate who command nearly everyone's respect. With the June 1 retirement of Siskiyou National Forest Supervisor Ron McCormick, we have one fewer.

In 1985, I made a public television documentary about the North Kalmiopsis Wilderness Area, probably the most controversial piece of real estate Ron (or any local public forester) had to manage. Much of this area burned two years later in the Silver Mountain Fire. But at the time it was a lush unentered forest that had environmental and timber activists at each others' throats.

I heard one theme over and over again as I interviewed people for that program: "Those extremists who don't agree with me," everyone seemed to be saying, "are selfish jerks who don't really care about the future of the forest or workers or Southern Oregon communities. They have nothing to say that needs to be heard." The one person who didn't tell me that in one way or another was Ron McCormick.

Managers in the kind of hot seat that Ron occupied tend to grab onto one set of dogma, put their hands down and plow forward. Ron never did that. He always remembered that wisdom about forest management comes from people holding a wide range of environmental viewpoints. He never forgot that everyone who yelled, pleaded, bullied or reasoned with

him were shareholders of his forests, people to whom he had a solemn responsibility of stewardship.

Ron's approach is the only kind that can steer us through the struggle over public forest management that lies ahead. We'll miss him.

JEFF GOLDEN
Medford

6/21/90

223

Conclusions

Editorials

Thanks for everything

Although he has put in 34 years, Siskiyou National Forest Supervisor Ron McCormick is likely to most remember the 6½ spent in southern Oregon after he retires today from the U.S. Forest Service.

As for those who knew McCormick and worked with him, they'll most certainly remember him — whether or not they always agreed with him — as a fair-minded man who put the forest first.

McCormick, 55, plans to remain in Grants Pass after his retirement, spending more time with his family and doing consulting work for a California-based organizational management firm.

The six-plus years he spent as head of the Siskiyou National Forest were years of controversy and confrontation. They were years during which the forest had to draft a new 10-year management plan, deal with the issue of a proposed Siskiyou National Park, prepare plans for the Silver fire timber salvage operation, and wrestle with the issues of logging in old-growth forests and protecting the spotted owl.

Those years tested McCormick's skills as a planner, manager and mediator. They tested his ability to work with people who had their own ideas about how the forest should be managed, people who usually weren't interested in hearing what the other side had to say or what Forest Service professionals thought.

To his lasting credit, McCormick never lost sight of the forest he managed. He refused to take sides, or to be drawn into dead-end confrontations. He listened, he explained, he did his homework. And then, time and time again, he did what he thought was best for the forest.

The Siskiyou National Forest's 10-year plan, among the first to be adopted, is a model in multiple-use planning. The Silver fire salvage plan, one of the most carefully drafted in Forest Service history, balanced the need to harvest blackened trees against the risks that logging might do added damage to the burned area.

McCormick doesn't get all the credit for the forest's success. He had some good people helping him out along the way. But he deserves a lot of it.

As supervisor, he set the tone for his agency. It was he who was open to looking at alternatives to traditional methods, including the "new forestry" approach to managing a forest for resources and biological diversity. It was he who was able to recognize that conflict is sometimes necessary to generate new ideas or confirm the validity of old ones.

We always found McCormick to be a straightforward, honest man. He had a job to do and did it to the best of his ability. We wish him the best of luck in the future, and we hope he hears more than just these few words of "thanks" today as he ends a stellar career. — R.A.S.

CHAPTER NINE

Movin' On...

The employees of the Siskiyou National Forest produced a retirement party that was as much a celebration of what we had accomplished together during the past seven years as it was a way to bid me farewell.

I realized that our shared experiences, as difficult and demanding as they often were – more often than not culminating in success – were a triumph of our collective spirit. I felt these seven years had been a once in a career event. I felt privileged and honored to have been associated with these fine people.

Our resident naturalist, Mary Paetzel, published a book in 1998 entitled *The Spirit of the Siskiyous*. It is a wonderful book about the special places of the forest, and the flowers, insects, birds and mammals that inhabit them. Now, years later, when I retrieve the book from our bookcase the title evokes memories of the people of the forest. They were also the 'Spirit of the Siskiyou'.

More than 150 people attended the celebration from all corners of the Siskiyou, adjoining forests, the regional office and the BLM. Some folks who had moved to positions of significant responsibility had returned for the party. I really felt good about the success they had attained. The reason for their success, of course, was due to their inherent ability and drive. However, I liked to think that their time and experience on the Siskiyou played a role.

John Berry became forest supervisor of the Eldorado Forest in California.

Ted Stubblefield, forest supervisor of the Olympic Forest, then the Gifford Pinchot Forest in Washington.

Bonnie Wood became forest supervisor of the Malheur Forest in Oregon.

Mike Ash became deputy regional forester for the Pacific Northwest Region.

Rich Stem became deputy regional forester for the Rocky Mountain Region.

Tom Riley became forest supervisor of the Clearwater Forest in Idaho.

One memento I received was a pen and ink sketch of a running pheasant. I had it framed and hung it on the wall by my desk at home. I cherish it. It displays the autographs of 120 employees and friends. It was drawn by Jerry Wildfong, who worked in the timber section of the supervisor's office. She was our unofficial forest artist. She did the artwork in most of the planning documents we produced and composed the infamous ballad, *Silver Sales*, which captured the drama of the Silver Fire and recovery project. Jerry was a creative and valuable employee.

Bob Ettner and Lee Webb created a slideshow which included photos of my early childhood, family members, early career and special events of the past seven years. The show was both entertaining and moving. All in all it was a fitting way to end my career with the U.S. Forest Service.

The employees' retirement gift to me was a top-brand mountain bike. Carol had suggested it to my secretary as I had talked about replacing my old 10-speed. It was a great gift! Most mornings I took a long ride around the valley, savoring the sights, sounds and smells of early summer, and gaining needed exercise. At those times I experienced an undeniable sense of freedom, and my heart would swell as I savored this new reality. I continue to ride the bike, but the distance has become a bit shorter.

In post retirement years I engaged in consulting work, first in team building and organizational development. I joined with my old compatriots Bruce Pewitt and Jack Dinwiddie in working with several national forests across the country in improving communications and performance of their management teams. I felt I had a lot to offer given my years of leadership on the Siskiyou.

It was a good experience for a couple of years, and paid well, but the setting was always a meeting room someplace, and the work very demanding. It required long, intensive hours working through sensitive and often personal employee issues.

City of Ashland Watershed Management Plan

The City of Ashland was seeking bids to develop a management plan for the Ashland Watershed. This key watershed provided the drinking water for their growing community. It is surrounded on three sides by the Rogue River National Forest. Water quality and fire risk were the main issues.

I spoke with my former associate and friend on the Siskiyou, John Hoffman (retired), about partnering on this project and submitting a bid. We did, and we were selected. We followed the Silver recovery model, with inventory of the conditions on the watershed, public participation, briefings, and we even formed a public advisory board. We developed and published a sound plan for protecting and managing the watershed, and we finished on schedule.

During this experience I found I really enjoyed the part about getting back on the ground in the role of forester and planner. I began to prepare stewardship plans for small tracts of privately owned forestlands. A federally funded program called the Stewardship Incentive Program is administered by the State Department of Forestry. The intent is to bring these small tracts under professional management.

A project usually involved finding property corners and locating property lines, inventorying and mapping the species and the condition of the stands of trees, and the condition of the streams.

Fieldwork! It took me back to my days as a neophyte forester and reminded me of why I became a forester in the first place. I thoroughly enjoyed it. I would spend a few days in the field inventorying and mapping the property, and then I would prepare a report and plan with specific recommendations (management prescriptions) to the landowner to protect and improve the stands of trees. The prescriptions typically involved thinning dense stands of fir and pine, reducing the amount of competing brush species, and planting trees.

At the landowner's request, I would obtain and supervise contractors to do the work. Under an approved stewardship plan, the landowner could be reimbursed a percentage of the cost of this work. I saw it as a win-win for both the landowner and the forested land. Over the next several years I probably did fifteen or more of these plans. It kept me in shape, at least met expenses, and most importantly got me into the forest again.

Rancho los Amigos – Baja

Carol and I had previously passed on an opportunity to purchase a lot in Baja Sur, Mexico. We learned that a beachfront lot was being resold and was available. Jack Dinwiddie quoted me a price.

The lot purchase plus the cost of construction for a vacation home was more than we could afford. It had to be all cash since mortgage loans were not available at that time in Baja, Mexico. So I called my brother Jerry, and his wife Dede, to see if they would be interested in partnering in this venture. Fortunately, they were. So we bought the lot, and over the years we developed a garage and a two-bedroom vacation home. We did a lot of the work ourselves.

Building in Mexico is tough. The regulations are not clear, the process is confusing and conditions difficult. Then there is the language barrier. The good part was that my brother and I were able to reconnect, work together on getting this project done, and discovered along the way how to coordinate our individual skills.

The story of Jack and John's development of Rancho los Amigos is well worth noting. Following the initial motorcycle trip of 1970 with Bruce and me, Jack made several more trips, camping in various parts of the Baja. He searched for a lot to buy that had a sound title. (One of the big problems with buying in Mexico is lack of title clarity.) With the help of a local rancher he found a piece of land between the old dirt road that paralleled the coast and the Sea of Cortez, located about twenty-five miles north of San Jose del Cabo. The owner, a rancher, would not sell just a lot, but would sell a larger piece of land.

Jack's dream expanded from buying a lot and cabin to a concept of subdividing several acres into lots and selling them to close friends, most of whom were or had been associated with the U.S. Forest Service, and creating a rustic Mexican ranch - Rancho los Amigos.

The scope of the project had grown exponentially, and so had the processes and problems. My brother is fond of saying, "Everything in Baja is a bargain, and you always get more than you bargained for." Jack enlisted the help of his realtor friend, John Hensley.

Together Jack and John made countless trips to Baja Sur and the town of San Jose Del Cabo, the local center of government. They fought and stumbled their way through the confusing and often contradicting rules and regulations of the local bureaucracies, which were (are) rife with corruption. They called it 'kicking the ball'. Each succeeding trip advanced the 'ball' a bit closer to the goal of subdividing and selling lots.

Eventually they got it done and sold lots to Bruce Pewitt and several other Forest Service friends, and built small homes on the beachfront. The community of Rancho los Amigos was born. Carol and I stay in our little 'casa' during early spring each year. The East

Cape of the Baja Peninsula is a study in contrasts, both physically and experientially. One day can bring a calm sea, light breezes, and the next a howling wind out of the north that can move sand horizontally along the beach. One morning can be spent fishing, swimming or kayaking, the next fixing the third flat of the week on our old vehicle, or chasing the propane delivery truck that passed us by without stopping as it sped down the dusty, washboard-ridden coast road, or searching for the guy that delivers the fresh water who was supposed to deliver three days ago.

At the age of sixty-five I was still doing stewardship plans for woodlot owners. I was often climbing very steep hills and fighting my way through heavy vegetation to inventory these properties. I fell a couple of times in steep, v-shaped canyons, and I had trouble getting back up and out of them. My knees began to protest and ached at night. I figured it was time to quit. Nothing lasts forever. One secret of a healthy retirement, I learned, is to stay active but face the reality of getting older, and to adjust my expectations and activities accordingly.

We later sold our wonderful home on three acres in Colonial Valley and moved into a compact home on a small lot on the edge of Grants Pass. It has been easier to take care of and facilitates worry-free traveling. The redeeming factor of this home is its location on the Rogue River.

Just this morning, after working on these memoirs for a couple of hours, I slipped on my waders and went out the back door for a couple of hours fishing for winter steelhead. That is worth a lot to me. A glance out the window at any time reveals mallards, wood ducks, Canada geese and, in the summer, osprey and a myriad of other birds. If we are lucky, we spot a muskrat, beaver or river otter.

In the fall I fish for the summer run steelhead. And therein lays a story.

Crossing the Rogue

The fall season in Southwest Oregon can be enchanting. The days parade by warm and sunny, with cool nights and crisp mornings. The Rogue River is resplendent in fall finery, with borders of gold, orange and red contributed to by the cottonwoods, alders and big leaf maples. The river environs are prepared to welcome home its wandering natives.

Chinook salmon, which have been ranging and feeding in the Pacific for several years, yield to a powerful instinct to convene in the bay at the mouth of the Rogue River just north of Gold Beach. They gather and wait. At some point, perhaps stimulated by a freshet of water from an early fall rain, they begin to make their migration upriver to the place they were born. They seek out traditional spawning beds that provide just the right mix of gravel size and river current to dig their nests, termed 'redds' by biologists.

We are fortunate to live on the river's edge and close to a large salmon spawning bed. I enjoy fishing for the summer steelhead that shadow the salmon on their upriver journey. Steelheads are a rainbow trout that also spend time at sea, and like their brother salmon return to the Rogue and its tributaries to spawn. They are a large, athletic fish, bright silver with a faint rainbow along their sides that hints of their river origin. They also have a taste for freshly laid salmon eggs.

I like to fish at daybreak and just below the spawning beds where the steelhead lay in wait for an easy breakfast of the occasional salmon egg that washes out of the redds. One of my favorite spots is a small midstream island that divides the river into two channels. To reach the island just before daylight means crossing the larger of the two channels in the dark. I make my way down a steep bank to the river's edge, fishing rod in one gloved hand and walking stick in the other. At my age I like the security of a walking stick when crossing. The river surface sliding quickly by, dimly reflecting the night sky like a black and silvery mirror, is beautiful but strangely disorienting.

As I enter the river I can just discern the dim outline of the island ahead. My stumbling and splashing disturbs a group of Canada geese roosting on the island, their talking and fussing reflects their increasing state of concern. With one final raucous and unanimous cackle, they fly off – an hour before their accustomed time.

To reach the island I must cross above a sizable riffle (some would consider it a rapid) that constitutes the larger channel. It emits an impressive roar as I near, reminding me this is not a good place to stumble and fall. It is awareness of the danger that sharpens my senses and spices up the adventure.

Sometimes I make the crossing with a fishing partner. We will often pause midstream just above the boiling whitewater to rest. The heavy current presses hard against my waders. We look at each other and grin. A couple of 'geezers' being kids again who understand and appreciate the moment. As we skirt the head of the riffle the water is thigh-high and fast. The pressure nudges me toward the lip of the riffle, which I resist. There is just enough dim light to make out where I need to go. I probe ahead with my booted toe, feeling for the next good foot-plant, and to locate and avoid the larger round rocks. At each step of my lead foot the current pushes it a few inches downriver, closer to the whitewater. The round, smooth, river bottom rocks are covered with stringy, brown algae, making them very slippery. Step by careful step we cross. Three quarters of the way we near the location of several salmon redds, and we avoid them. The salmon leave their redds at dark to rest and perhaps sleep in deeper, slower water. Occasionally we will startle a pair of fish that have returned early to their redd. Chinook are big fish, often over three feet long and weighing up to fifty pounds. They explode in a churning, boiling wake looking like a couple of motorboats as they speed away. I am as startled as they are, and my heart jumps!

We reach the island as dawn is breaking and get ready to fish. Sometimes, if you are patient and observant, the river offers a gift. Perhaps a kingfisher diving from above for a crawdad, or if you are fortunate, a curious otter moving quickly among the rocks on the far bank to check out the intruder and then make a hasty exit. This time I watched a shift change of the herons. A black-crowned night heron passes overhead, leaving its river fishing spot to roost for the day in his favorite cottonwood; and shortly thereafter, a great blue heron lands awkwardly on the bank just downriver, joining us for a morning of fishing. Oh, yes. Once in a while I am fortunate to hook a beautiful, fighting steelhead.

It is good to be retired.

Ron and Mike atop Mt. Borah, Idaho 12,662 feet, 8/14/01

Fishing the Sea of Cortez

Baja Casa

EPILOGUE

Not long ago I was reading the Sunday paper on our back deck and casually watching the Rogue River flow by. It was a sunny, pleasant morning in early October, and the water was low and clear. A few wary wood ducks were searching for a meal along the river's edge. The heavy fall rains were still a few weeks away.

I noticed a dark shape in the languid water. Looking closer I realized it was a salmon, a huge fall Chinook. This was clearly a female; one that had recently completed spawning in the traditional spawning beds a short distance upriver – her long journey over and duty completed.

I put the paper down and watched as she swam languidly along, fighting a tendency to roll on her side. It was clear to me that her energy was nearly spent. Her recent adventures of outrunning sea lions at the river's mouth, fighting her way up the hundred miles of rushing river and, after several attempts, leaping her way up and over Rainie Falls had burned much of her stored body fat. Her remaining energy had been expended digging her redd, turning on her side and flailing her body against the rocky river bed to create a depression, rubbing her skin raw in the process, and then finally depositing her eggs.

All this had taken a terrible toll. The once magnificent, silver body of the king of the salmon had deteriorated to a dull, mottled gray, with patches of a white fungus that had invaded the tears and abrasions.

She didn't give up easily. She drifted on her side for a few moments, her gill plates still pumping oxygenated water through the blood-rich filaments of her gills. With one final effort and tail stroke, she momentarily righted herself, only to roll over again. Belly up, head bumping along the rocky bottom, she gently floated downriver and out of sight.

There was no ceremony, no celebration of her achievements and life – only my admiration and sadness.

I remained for a while, gripped by a melancholy inconsistent with this beautiful morning on the river. And I knew why.

It had been nearly twenty years since I had retired, and Carol and I were enjoying life. I had experienced the joy of becoming a grandpa, and the shock and implications of becoming a great-grandfather. Then there has been the travel and freedom to choose for each day, week or month what we wished to do – the wonderful gifts of senior years.

However, during that period, I had also witnessed the slow dismantling of the Siskiyou National Forest, and the near disappearance of the Forest Service in our community of Grants Pass. The drastically curtailed level of timber harvest was accompanied by shrinking budgets. In order to reduce expenses, the Siskiyou and the Rogue River National Forests were combined and co-located within the Bureau of Land Management office in Medford. The five ranger districts of the Siskiyou had been combined into three. There was less than half the complement of personnel compared to 1990. This scenario was not unique to the Siskiyou. It was being replicated across the United States in nearly every national forest.

Just as it was hard for me to watch the slow passing of that courageous and dedicated Chinook salmon, so has it been to witness the inexorable decline of the outfit to which I had dedicated a good portion of my life, always respected and now revered.

I sat quietly on our deck on this beautiful fall morning and reviewed in my mind the events that I thought had led to today's reality for the Forest Service.

We just didn't listen closely. We did not pay close attention to the signals. We sensed, but did not acknowledge an undercurrent of public discontent. We didn't respond quickly or forcefully. The public's message was there in many forms: appeals, lawsuits, and even legislation. And the forests themselves were reinforcing that message.

A brief and vastly oversimplified chronology might be helpful at this point. In the late 1800s there was growing concern that the remaining timberlands in the country were going to be cutover following the popular practice of 'cut and run'. The great forests of the Eastern United States had already been cutover for fast profits, sold and converted to fields for agriculture. The pine forests of the Southeast followed suite, and a similar fate appeared inevitable for the West. At the same time, congress awoke to the fact that forests and wood products had been an important element in the development of the United States, and would likely continue to be. Amid growing concern over shrinking forests in 1891, congress authorized the president to set aside forest reserves from the remaining public domain.

The Organic Act followed in 1897 and specified purposes for these forest reserves, and provided for their protection and administration. In 1905 the Forest Service was created and given authority to enforce law and regulations on the new reserves. Gifford Pinchot was named the first chief forester. In 1907 the forest reserves were renamed national forests. The utilitarian concept of managing forests for sustained yield was taking root. Chief Pinchot coined the term 'conservation' – the wise use of forests and all natural resources. Those focused on short-term profit were angry over this turn of events. Those with a longer-term view were delighted. To many, forest rangers became heroes.

The Multiple Use-Sustained Act of 1960 directed the Forest Service to give equal weight and consideration to outdoor recreation, range, timber, water, wildlife and fish. I recall I was in the Calaveras Ranger District Office shortly thereafter, and I saw and heard District Ranger Bill Lunsford who, with a broad smile, told his staff that this was a great event in the history of the national forests.

A great cheer rose from the ranks across the national forests. Perhaps the primacy of timber was ending. Perhaps funding for programs would be more equitable and in line with public wishes. Slowly there was acknowledgement and greater consideration for the value of these other forest resources. But the timber interests kept the pressure on their representatives in government. In the end, timber continued to receive the dominant emphasis.

The Wilderness Act of 1964, the National Environmental Policy Act (NEPA) of 1970, and the 1976 National Forest Management Act (NFMA) all reflected the public's evolving preferences for managing the national forests; and clearly it was not that timber considerations were primary.

In the view of environmental groups, nothing much had changed on the ground, and their collective frustration continued to grow unabated.

Then in 1992 at the Earth Summit in Rio de Janeiro, Forest Service Chief Dale Robertson announced that clear-cutting would no longer be the major harvest method on the forests. He also stated an ecosystem approach to managing the forests was now an official policy. Now that was a courageous act, and harbinger of great change.

In 1994 the Northwest Forest Plan was approved by President Clinton. Thousands of acres were taken out of the timber base and set aside for spotted owl habitat; the owl had just previously been declared a threatened species. The annual sale quantities in many western national forests were cut by two-thirds. Budgets and the number of personnel dropped accordingly. Environmentalists rejoiced.

All of this formative legislative activity was done in a period marked by conflict, intrigue, political infighting and maneuvering. Controversy remained the hallmark of the creation and the continued existence of the Forest Service.

The wheel of natural resource fortune had been given a mighty spin by the Clinton administration. It sped by the peg on the board representing balance in resource considerations. The delicate balance that many Forest Service folks and I sought for so many years was bypassed as inconsequential.

The wheel's indicator stopped dead on the preservation peg. The mission of the Forest Service had been abruptly and without ceremony changed to ecosystem perpetuation and protection of biodiversity. I concluded this had probably been inevitable.

I did not like the notion of timber being the primary value of a national forest, and for thirty years of my career I resisted that notion. I am also uncomfortable with the dramatic shift to preservation as the primary value, even though I understand how we arrived there.

If you had the patience to follow the journey of this quiet kid from Northeast Ohio, whose love of the outdoors led him from Ober's woods to fieldwork (real forestry), then into a maelstrom of controversy, political intrigue and intervention, you might wonder that our system works at all. Some say chaos is just part of the democratic process. Others conclude our system is often counterproductive. I had witnessed a lot of both.

I described the Hells Canyon NRA planning task that involved genuine and intensive public participation and months of hard work to hammer out agreements between key interest groups, only to have it all negated and reversed by a change in administrations and the stroke of the pen of a newly appointed Assistant Secretary of Agriculture.

The scream of 'foul' reverberates today from the mighty walls of Hells Canyon. The publics that participated felt duped. My planning team felt humiliated and betrayed.

Then I described in some detail the effort by the dedicated folks of the Siskiyou National Forest to produce a well balanced Forest Land and Resource Management Plan and, in spite of the last-minute intervention by the governor, we did that. Following a national election the political parties changed and in an early action of the new Clinton administration, the Siskiyou Plan and those of other national forests in Washington and Oregon were largely discarded. The new plan was called the Presidents Plan, later renamed the Northwest National Forest Plan. It leaned strongly to preservation as opposed to management.

The Multiple Use Sustained Yield Act of 1960 that held so much promise was disappointing in its implementation. NEPA of 1970 was helpful but not conclusive, and the NFMA of 1976 was politically marginalized. But the President's plan brought about the watershed event, the sea change that I long sensed was coming had finally arrived.

The Plan prescribed a new mission of preserving ecosystem integrity and biodiversity, i.e. ecosystem management. As enlightened as that may be, I believe it contained a glaring weakness. This new plan left little room for research and exploration on how to extract wood fiber within these new constraints.

It has been my observation that the further apart the ideologies of our two great political parties grew, the more determined was each to have everything their way. That trend seems to have intensified and amplified over time. From taxes to healthcare to foreign policy to policy governing our nation's public land natural resources, a new administration's ideology was forced onto the country. In the case of natural resources, the overriding interest became not their best protection and wise use, but whose political philosophy would dominate and control policy, decisions and the budget.

Both parties seemed to forget or ignore that protection and management of public lands and natural resources is a long-term proposition, certainly longer than one or two presidential terms.

I am not judging one political party or the other, but I am critical of our system, and the effect it has had on responsible public land and resource management. During my career I watched, close up, as our political parties with diametrically opposed political philosophies and agendas wreak havoc with local natural resource planning, and ultimately with the spirit of conservation itself. It could and probably will happen again.

A Proposal

We need to find a way to provide a rational consistency over the long term. My conclusion is that our great country, blessed with an abundance of natural resources, would benefit if our public land and resource management agencies could be insulated from the fickle winds of politics. The objective would be to temper political ideology with professional experience and judgment and prevent frequent and abrupt changes in direction.

I have long held the view that if our government formed a Federal Public Land and Resources Board, it could become a shield between the agencies, congress and the administration.

The Federal Public Land and Resources Board would include a cadre of top-ranked and esteemed ecologists, wildlife and fisheries biologists, foresters, soil scientists, and the best minds in the field from academia. They could come from the ranks, both active and retired, of natural resource management agencies, and universities across the country.

They would be appointed for defined terms by the president and vetted by the Senate. They would be an independent body, similar to the Federal Reserve. Their role would be to:

1. Analyze the morass of conflicting laws that govern public land protection and management and develop a plan for congress to remedy this untenable situation.
2. Develop, coordinate and guide the nation's natural resource and public land management policies to ensure long-term ecological health and conservation of the nation's wealth of national treasures.
3. Guide the budget process for submittal to congress of a rational budget for the protection and management of public land and resources.
4. Maintain oversight of public natural resource and land management agencies, and provide a credible and objective buffer between them and the vagaries of our political process.

I believe that with a renewed sense of mission and a little farsighted assistance from the congress, the Forest Service can and will survive.

The destiny of the mighty Chinook salmon is predetermined, a fate locked into its genetic makeup. The Forest Service, however, time and time again throughout its history has demonstrated the capacity to reinvent itself.

Some interpret the current struggles of our beloved outfit as death throes. I think of them as the effort of yet another metamorphosis. I believe the destiny of the Forest Service is to once again emerge as the preeminent natural resource protection and management agency in the world, seizing the lead on implementing its redefined mission of 'caring for the land and serving the people'.

It is our legacy.